Transition to Success

Transition to Success

Training Students to Lead Peer Groups in Higher Education

Melinda S. Harper, PhD
Christine L. Allegretti, PhD

MP MOMENTUM PRESS
HEALTH

Transition to Success: Training Students to Lead Peer Groups in Higher Education
Copyright © Momentum Press®, LLC, 2018.

First published 2018 by
Momentum Press®, LLC
222 East 46th Street, New York, NY 10017
www.momentumpress.net

ISBN-13: 978-1-94664-606-4 (print)
ISBN-13: 978-1-94664-607-1 (e-book)

Momentum Press Psychology Collection

DOI: 10.5643/978194664671

Cover and interior design by S4Carlisle Publishing Services
Private Ltd., Chennai, India

Frist edition: 2018

10 9 8 7 6 5 4 3 2 1

Printed in the United States of America

Abstract

Using students as peer leaders, mentors, supporters, and sources of information for other students, especially first-year students, is an established practice among higher-education institutions. These student leaders are especially influential at creating a social community for first-year students. However, many student leaders in these important roles are not provided with the necessary training to develop, lead, and maintain a connected and cohesive peer group. This book provides readers with a guide for selecting, training, and supervising students as leaders of a first-year student peer group, the Transition to University program. The book also includes theories and techniques specific to group dynamics and leadership skills as well as a format for a supervision course for students serving as peer leaders.

Keywords

College student adjustment, peer leaders, student leaders, peer mentors, first-year student adjustment, group dynamics, leadership training, transition to university

Contents

Preface

Peers have a significant impact on normative young adult psychological development. In particular, peer support is powerful in promoting success in the higher-education setting. The normative developmental transition from high school to college is fraught with a myriad of challenges and tasks, and the influence of peers on each other during this developmental stage can be integral to successful outcomes. Using peers as influential leaders, supporters, and mentors in the educational process of other students has been a recognized and common practice among higher-education institutions (Brack, Millard, & Shah, 2008; Carns, Carns, & Wright, 1993; Collier, 2015; Cuseo, 2010a; Newton & Ender, 2010, among others). Not only are peer leaders economical resources for the university, they are also relatable, experienced, and effective with their fellow students (Lockspeiser, O'Sullivan, Teherani, & Muller, 2008). University students play a number of peer leader roles on campus providing direct support including admission ambassadors, orientation leaders, resident advisors, peer mentors, peer counselors, peer learning community assistants, and alumni mentors. Peer leaders also play a role as peer teachers, who may serve as tutors, supplemental instruction leaders, writing fellows, student instructors, or fellows in first-year seminars. In addition, peer leaders may be engaged as retention agents by conveying to their fellow students the advantages and opportunities the institution distinctively offers (Cuseo, 2010c).

Student leaders can be especially influential in assisting their first-year student peers with developing new social groups. Positive affiliations and strong relationships with those on campus can profoundly impact the new students' ability to succeed not only with the transition to their university life but also throughout their academic career (Mattanah, 2016). The strategic and intentional formation of small groups during this transitional process provides a social community and network that fills the normative void experienced by university students upon leaving their own communities and arriving at a new one. A solution for this problem is to assist first-year university students with creating new attachments that mirror or resemble previous important relationships. Student leaders can enable the formation of this new, cohesive social community rather than merely serving primarily as sources of information or one-on-one support. These leaders can initiate and foster the development of a new social microsystem that assists their fellow entering students with navigating the normative stressors experienced when transitioning to university life. With structured training, advanced students can learn the interpersonal and leadership skills that will be useful during their university experience as well as being a benefit throughout life.

The Scope of This Book

In this book, we focus on students in higher education and their development as peer leaders within an organized social group experience. We emphasize using groups in particular given the multiple advantages offered in this type of context. Specifically, the group setting offers a normalizing and universally shared atmosphere where group members' experiences are mirrored by each other. In addition, the group context offers a convenient way to provide education and support to several individuals at once. Finally, groups offer the opportunity to hear and learn different perspectives in a safe and shared space.

We organized this book into sections that outline the selection and training of students as peer leaders of their own peer support group. In Chapter 1, we present a brief review of the use of students as peer leaders in higher education. Chapter 2 focuses on group dynamics as it relates to peer groups. Chapters 3 and 4 detail the necessary training student leaders will need to lead their own peer groups. Chapters 5 and 6 focus on the coleader relational dynamic and specific techniques student leaders can implement when leading a peer support group. Chapter 7 presents a brief overview of the T2U program at Queens University of Charlotte as an applied example of how to use student peer leaders in a supportive social group setting. Chapter 8 describes a practicum-based course to provide ongoing supervision and training of student leaders. Finally, Chapter 9 offers implications and an introduction to a more detailed program (T2U) that will be outlined in Book 2 of this series.

Acknowledgments

Many thanks to the people who have helped in the completion of this book. First, thank you to our reviewers, colleagues, and friends. We especially want to thank Melissa Bodford, Dr. Rick Deitchman, Scott Fouts, Dr. Richard Goode, Jaime Hollerbach, Dr. Dorothy Roberts, Amy Scharf, and Allan Shub. They generously gave of their time and efforts to discuss and read our manuscript, and their feedback was invaluable in the final edition of this work.

We also extend gratitude to the helpful staff at Momentum Press for their support and guidance toward the completion of this book.

We also express sincere appreciation and acknowledgement to those who have supported the T2U program, both at Queens University of Charlotte and at other institutions. In particular, we are especially grateful to Dr. S. Mark Pancer for his generous support, time, and expertise in developing the T2U program at Queens University of Charlotte.

Finally, we appreciate our spouses and families for their love and support throughout this endeavor.

CHAPTER 1

Students as Peer Leaders

The concept of mentoring, or the relationship between peers in supportive roles, can be traced back to the first recorded use of the term in *The Odyssey* (Roberts, 1999). Homer described Odysseus' old friend, Mentor, who provided guidance to Telemachus while Odysseus was away fighting the Trojan War (Homer, trans. 1996). Mentor was less than successful in his role of overseeing Telemachus and the household that was overrun by suitors for Telemachus' mother and Odysseus' wife, Penelope, during Odysseus' long absence. The goddess Athena frequently disguised herself in the form of Mentor and interceded to guide and protect Telemachus while Odysseus was away at war.

The modern concept of mentor was developed and given attributes that are more like our current interpretation of the word by Fenelon in 1699 in *Les Adventures de Telemaque* (Roberts, 1999). In this story, according to Roberts (1999), Mentor was given the role of providing Telemachus with support, guidance, and advice. This role of a mentor supports the modern concept of a relationship that develops among individuals and provides support and guidance through transitional issues in a hierarchical relationship with the mentor being considerably older and wiser. More recently, mentoring relationships have been developed between individuals in peer relationships, such as higher-education settings. This current concept of peer mentoring in higher education focuses on more near-peer relationships with the mentor being of approximately the same age but having more academic and social/emotional experience. Terrion and Leonard (2007) describe this mentoring relationship as "a helping relationship in which two individuals of similar age and/or experience come together, either informally or through formal mentoring schemes, in the pursuit of fulfilling some combination of functions that are career-related (e.g., information sharing, career strategizing) and psychosocial (e.g., confirmation, emotional support, personal feedback, friendship)" (p.150). These roles are commonly referred to as mentor, educator, and leader, among other terms. Of these peer support roles, Cuseo (2010b) suggested that peer leader is the most comprehensive term to describe the one-to-one supportive relationship that develops. In addition to the support and guidance of a peer mentor, peer leaders also support academic and social development. Cuseo also proposed that peer leaders may be a role model, a personal support agent, and a resource and referral agent. In this critical role, peer leaders can influence a variety of outcomes, including academic, college, and life success.

Roles of Peer Leaders

Peer leaders perform a variety of functions or roles when interacting with students. These roles fit into broad categories: providing social and emotional support, facilitating career and professional development, and role modeling successful behavior (Jacobi, 1991). Peer leaders serve as a model of a successful student by demonstrating academic success, appropriate time management, and social involvement on campus. Moreover, peer mentors provide the cultural capital that helps students to succeed (Collier, 2015). When students understand the expectations both from the courses that they take and in the academic setting in general, they can be more successful.

A peer leader serving a role in any of the above areas may potentially impact a mentee's success in higher education. A number of conditions related to the student experience with the institution have been identified as related to student success. Among these factors associated with student success are active academic and social involvement (Astin, 1977; Cuseo, 2007), self-efficacy (Cuseo, 2007; Tinto, 2016), academic and social support (Tinto, 1999; Upcraft, Gardner, & Barefoot, 2007), and sense of belonging in which students are able "to find at least one smaller community of students with whom they share a common bond" (Tinto, 2016, para.11).

Outcomes of Peer-based Programs

Research consistently indicates positive outcomes of peer mentoring in multiple areas of student functioning at the university or higher educational level (Collier, 2015; Cuseo, 2010a). For example, first-year students who participated in a peer support group led by upper-class university students returned for their sophomore year at a significantly higher percentage compared to first-year students who did not participate in the peer-based program (Harper & Allegretti, 2009a; 2013; Pancer, Pratt, Hunsberger, & Alisat, 2004). In addition, students who received peer support achieved better academic performance as indicated by a higher grade point average compared to those who were not connected with a peer mentor (Asgari & Frederick, 2016; Hughes, 2011; Mattanah, Brooks, Brand, Quimbly, & Ayers, 2012; Thile & Matt, 1995). Moreover, areas of psychosocial functioning including self-efficacy, social support, and emotional growth were positively associated with peer support (Harper & Allegretti, 2009b; Mattanah, Ayers, Brand, Brooks, Quimby, and McNary, 2010; Pratt et al., 2000; Terrion & Leonard, 2007; Thile & Matt, 1995) as were lower levels of loneliness (Mattanah et al., 2010). Finally, peer support has been associated with overall satisfaction with the institution and increased ability to connect with campus resources and deal with adjustment issues (Beatrice & Shively, 2007; Collier, 2015; Sanchez, Bauer, & Paronto, 2006).

Peer leaders also benefit from the leadership role of mentoring a fellow student (Harper & Allegretti, 2015). Specifically, peer leaders gain a more in-depth understanding of their academic discipline and enhance their leadership and communication skills (Smith, 2013). In addition, peer mentors report an increase in confidence with their own skills and ability to teach within their discipline (Dennison, 2010).

Types of Peer-based Programs

Programs that use peer leaders to help educate students in higher education cover topics from educational and service activities to personal enrichment (Newton & Ender, 2010). For example, curricular peer mentoring programs offer supplemental instruction or peer-assisted learning in a specific course or discipline, such as gateway courses for majors or first-year seminars, to enhance the pedagogical experience (Greenfield, Keup, & Gardner, 2013; Smith, 2013). The interaction focuses on the relationship between the peer leader and the individual student, small groups, or large groups. The objective is to bolster academic skills, although social support and adjustment are the possible by-products of the interaction with the peer leader. The group setting is most successful because of its potential not only to encourage interactions with the leader but also to enhance social connection and interaction among the other mentees (Smith, 2013). Research indicates that participation in peer leadership programs where the peer mentors serve as supplemental instructors has been associated with academic outcomes such as higher-grade performance (Asgari & Frederick, 2016; Hughes, 2011).

Peer-based programs have targeted a variety of student populations in transition, including veterans (Erickson, 2015), first-generation low-income students, international students (Braun & Townley, 2015), minority students (Thile & Matt, 1995), and community college students transferring to the university setting (Collier, 2015). Additional programs have also successfully focused on psychological outcomes such as anxiety (Walker & Verklan, 2016) and disordered eating (Becker, Bull, Schaumberg, Cauble, & Franco, 2008; Becker, Smith, Ciao, 2006).

Peer-based programs whose goals are to facilitate and support the first-year student transitioning to higher education are common in colleges and universities. For example, orientation programs have a long history of using students as leaders to help with the transition to university life. Orientation leaders, or OLs, assist groups of students not only with academic goals that can include explaining the academic expectations, but also with social goals that can help build community and a sense of the campus culture (Greenfield et al., 2013).

An example of an extended orientation peer mentoring program that emphasizes the one-on-one connection between a peer mentor and a new student is the program at Wilkes University in Wilkes-Barre, PA (Ruthkosky & Castano, 2007). As part of their first-year student orientation program, each new student is paired with a peer leader three months before the beginning of the fall semester as a way to ease the anxiety of new students and provide information to them. The peer mentors send a letter to their mentees that introduces them to an online mentoring forum where the students can ask advice and participate in discussing topics of common concern for first-year students before the beginning of the first term. The peer mentors also initiate discussions of topics of general interest such as roommate issues, campus activities, and time management. The peer mentors also serve as orientation leaders when the new students arrive on campus. In this role, they lead "icebreaker" activities, work with the students in a community service project, and attend group advising meetings. This program of e-mentoring continues through the fall semester and may take place face-to-face. Of the modes of mentoring, the face-to-face was preferred by the mentees. They reported that the program eased their transition by helping their social adjustment, providing academic advice and support, and introducing them to campus resources.

Another example of successful individual mentoring that extends beyond the fall semester of the first year is the program at Humboldt State University (Ortiz & Virnoche, 2015). In this program, peer mentors were undergraduate and graduate students who met individually with each of their 25 mentees 10–12 times over the two semesters of their first year. The topics the mentors discussed in the meetings were timed to address common stressors that occurred during the semester (e.g., homesickness in September and midterm stress in October). Additionally, the mentors discussed other normative personal issues including family concerns, physical health, substance use, and finances. This mentoring experience also provided opportunities to discuss majors, explore careers, and outline a four-year plan. Results following the first-year pilot program indicated an increase in retention rates when compared to a five-year average prior to the program.

A different modality of peer mentoring uses small groups led by student leaders. The strategic and intentional formation of small groups within this transitional process maximizes the likelihood of students successfully adjusting to their new university life. Since connecting with a small group of students on campus can increase the likelihood of the students' persistence at the institution (Tinto, 2016), small groups on campus can provide first-year students with a social community that can ideally fill the void left by leaving their own communities. The Transition to University program, or T2U, at Queens University of Charlotte exemplifies this approach. The T2U program uses students as peer leaders to direct, guide, and provide support for first-year students throughout the first year, giving the vertical support from the older and more experienced student. In addition, the group simultaneously develops into a peer support system for the individual first-year student members, thus serving to develop the horizontal support for the group as well. In this way, the group's vertical support from the experienced peer leaders acts as the scaffolding that gives support to the group members through mature guidance and expert information, as well as empathy and critical thinking skills for problem-solving. The group's horizontal support builds over time and allows the gradual development of new friendships among the group members to help fill the void created when the students leave the safety and comfort of their old friends at home. Over the course of the first year, the group begins to take on key characteristics of a functioning and cohesive group, including identification with each other, participation in a shared system and experience, a collective sense of unity, and a shared interest in pursuit of goals (Cartwright & Zander, 1968). Universities that have implemented the T2U program have found significant positive results related to the first-year students' adjustment (Harper & Allegretti, 2009a; 2013; Mattanah et al., 2010; Pancer et al., 2004, Pratt et al., 2000). Student leaders are poised to make a positive impact through peer-based programs. They can model successful academic and social behaviors as well as provide relevant information. However, the degree of their success depends upon the student leaders' training. A basic understanding of the group dynamic process and ongoing, systematic supervision are essential for student leaders to be as successful and impactful as possible in a peer-based program.

CHAPTER 2

The Group Dynamic Process

Affiliation with a group is a core element of the human experience and is understood to be essential to human survival (Barchas, 1986; Baumeister & Leary, 1995; Buss, 1990, 1991). Considered vital for normative, healthy human development, this connection offers multiple positive benefits, including reducing emotional distress and physical symptoms of stress, increasing self-esteem, and enhancing positive social identity (Crocker & Luhtanen, 1990; Hale, Hannum, & Espelage, 2005; Hefner & Eisenburg, 2009; Tajel & Turner, 1979; Tajel, 1981).

Associations with large gatherings of people do not necessarily constitute affiliation with or belonging to a group. Being part of a group in and of itself possesses unique, specific elements that differentiate it from superficial associations based on generic characteristics, such as physical proximity (e.g., employees who share office space). These characteristics include constant interplay between the group members' interdependence, communication interactions, goal achievement, member roles, and group norms and rules (Cartwright & Zander, 1968; Homans, 1950; Levine & Moreland, 1994; McGrath, 1984).

In general, groups evolve over time (Mennecke, Hoffer, & Wynne, 1992; Moreland & Levine, 1988). They are fluid and sensitive in nature both to the individualistic and to the universal group tendencies as well as the attitudes and behaviors of their members and leaders. As such, the group follows a unique developmental trajectory that depends upon a myriad of competing and interconnecting influences. Historically, research theories attempting to organize this evolving dynamic differentiate between two primary types of approaches: sequential-stage theories and recurring-phase theories.

Sequential-stage theories are the traditional paradigm approach to understanding group development and dynamics. These theories place an emphasis on a typical or expected order of phases (Moreland & Levine, 1988; Worchel, Coutant-Sassic, & Grossman, 1992; Wheelan, 2005). Perhaps, the best known sequential-stage theory is the model proposed by Tuckman (1965). Tuckman and Jensen (1977) revised the original model to include five specific stages of group development: Forming, Storming, Norming, Performing, and Adjourning.

According to Tuckman and Jensen's model (1977), a distinctive group dynamic characterizes each of the five stages. In the Forming stage of group development, group members experience a normative sense of "awkwardness" and anxiety as they begin to learn how the group works and how they will "fit in" with the rest of the group. The uncertainty of this novel experience and early relationships with other group members activates a premature dependence upon any indicators of formal structure or rules that help to identify socially acceptable behaviors and expectations of participating group members. A notable distinction of this phase is a clear reliance on the instruction and direction of the group leader(s). Successful transition to the next stage is dependent upon a number of factors, including the time devoted to a specific task, interpersonal styles of more extroverted group members, and skilled group leaders who effectively set the stage and tone for what develops for the group as a whole.

As group members progress to the Storming stage, they can expect to feel a normative increase in tension and conflict within the group. This change in group dynamic, and in the group's progressive development, relates to two key factors: 1) an increase in shared space and time as a group, and 2) an increased willingness on the part of group members to take healthy risks in sharing their individual perspectives and personalities with the group. As the social façade of politeness and superficial connection fades, more authentic and honest exchanges and feedback begin to emerge. The group becomes a social microcosm for each group member; moreover, it morphs into an extended reality of their outside world. As such, interpersonal styles and maladaptive patterns that present outside of the group will appear in the group as well. Naturally, these emerging facets of group members result in increased intragroup conflict and ultimately an opportunity for the group to grow together. This conflict is not mandatory or intolerable; in fact, some groups may experience it to a minor degree or not at all. However, groups that do experience this stage to some degree gain the opportunity to practice and work through successful conflict resolution and genuine connection with a rich and diverse group of people who are invested in the group's goals and outcomes. Assisted by group leaders who model healthy communication and conflict negotiation, the process thrives. During this Storming stage, the group as a whole may experience an opportunity to undergo an emotional encounter characterized by reality testing, interaction, and support that assists in developing the connection of the group members (Frank & Asher, 1951; Yalom and Leszcz, 2005).

Following the growth of the group in the Storming stage, group members in the Norming stage experience a sense of cohesion and commitment to the group that includes accepting the unique perspectives and behaviors each individual offers to the group as a whole. Members acknowledge that these differences enhance the group, and this recognition brings a sense of harmony, belonging, and "we"-ness to the group process as well as feelings of trust and comfort (Fuhriman & Burlingame, 1990; Tuckman, 1965; Wheelan, 2005). One essential piece of this transitional stage between Storming and Performing is the agreement to the norms, or agreed upon group rules and expectations. During the Norming stage, a foundational commitment and understanding of the group develops and may include the establishment of procedural or interaction norms among group members (Engleberg & Wynn, 2013).

Building upon the successful development of the group through the first three stages, the fluidity of participation and process as a group comes together in the Performing stage. The goal is now to accomplish what is best for the group as a whole. Conflicts may still emerge; however, the group collectively and effectively modulates the tension and resolves the issue quickly with minimal disruption to bring the focus back to the group as cohesive unit. Processing happens openly and actively within the group rather than being minimized or avoided now that the interpersonal structure evident in the early stages provides an effective framework to rely upon.

Finally, in the Adjourning stage, the group members gradually grow aware that the group experience and connection will eventually conclude. While this awareness activates normative anxiety, sadness, and even disengagement for group members who have invested energy and resources toward forming and stabilizing of the group, this stage also yields an opportunity for self-reflection, feedback, and appreciation for the growth and contributions this shared experience has offered. This important stage requires adequate time to assist group members with the ending of, and transitioning, from the group. Resolution of this stage may come in the form of concluding observations about the group's overall process, gratitude toward group members for participating and respecting each other, and essential lessons that could be applied in the future.

In contrast to the sequential-stage theories, recurring-phase theories suggest that groups are characterized by having distinct issues that will continuously impact the group dynamic. These issues are subject to recurrence throughout the life of the group (Bion, 1961; Schultz, 1966). Change and movement are an accepted part of the group's fluid development and progress. Although individuals bring their own unique idiosyncrasies and contributions to the group, a much larger system and process is at play. The group process operates as more than just an exchange of question-response and a dyadic back-and-forth while progressing through sequential, methodical phases; rather, the process involves a complex, interactive web of verbal and nonverbal behaviors whereby "group members' behavior is simultaneously moving in all directions at once, a continuous series of circular loops or recurring chains of influence" (Goldenberg & Goldenburg, 2013, p.22). The group develops cohesion and purpose over time, but the progression is neither predictable nor linear in manner.

In reality, student leaders can expect to experience the interplay of the sequential and recurring phases of group development. While there are key stages that offer student leaders a guideline for progressing toward cohesion, leaders must also be mindful that the group dynamic actively evolves and may even return to a previously experienced stage of group development. For example, introducing a new group member or other positive disruptions to the sequential development may activate feelings and perceptions reminiscent of an earlier stage, such as Storming. This recurring phase need not be interpreted as regression or a decline in the group's development; rather, it serves as an opportunity for the group to grow.

CHAPTER 3

The Peer Leadership Process

Effective leadership is one of the most essential elements in groups and a prerequisite for the direction and integration of group members toward a common goal. Effective leaders are especially necessary for social affiliations and other related groups to succeed and thrive. However, leadership in and of itself is one of the most misunderstood and confusing nuances in the human experience (Bennis, 1975; Burns, 1978; Gardner, 1990). This misunderstanding may arise partly from the ever constant evolution, change, and shifts in dynamics inherent in the leadership process. Current leadership experts emphasize not only identifying values of leadership but also developing an understanding and knowledge of strategic leadership techniques (Boyatzis and McKee, 2005; Goleman, Boyatzis, & McKee, 2002; Hibberd, Smith, & Wylie, 2006). The operating premise for leadership success now assumes that members of the group or team are invested contributors to the overall goal rather than merely unchallenging and willing followers. This change in perspective from the control of others to empowering the group as a whole is an important shift for leaders to understand. From this perspective, the leader's success is measured by the process used to achieve the goals.

Student peer-based programs create an ideal arena for leadership training. The success of the group is predicated upon its facilitators possessing not only the appropriate characteristics and abilities to maintain the responsibilities of effective leaders, but also receiving the appropriate training and skillset to engage and connect the group members effectively. In addition, selection and pairing of group facilitators can encourage the social climate and cohesion of the group.

Leadership Characteristics of Peer Mentors

A peer mentor serves as a role model who is credible, trustworthy, and has expertise (Collier, 2015). In their review of the career-related factors and psychosocial functions of peer mentors, Terrion and Leonard (2007) identified effective characteristics of peer mentors. For example, one career-related characteristic of the peer mentoring relationship, the field of study, results in the mentee being more satisfied with the relationship if mentor and mentee pursued the same field of study. In addition, Terrion and Leonard (2007) also identified specific psychosocial characteristics important to effective peer relationships including good communication skills, interdependent attitude, flexibility, cultural proficiency, trustworthiness, and supportiveness. Students are typically enthusiastic and motivated to take on leadership roles; however, these characteristics alone do not necessarily translate to the actual abilities and capabilities of an effective student leader. Student leaders must convey a variety of intrapersonal and interpersonal characteristics essential to leading in a way that maximizes the group's overall potential and success. An ideal student leader demonstrates emotional and cognitive maturity and a proven history of achieving goals, time management, and self-regulation. These leaders are open to critiques and invite feedback for the benefit of improving and learning. Moreover, ideal student leaders demonstrate a willingness to give and to self-sacrifice for the benefit of the group.

The interpersonal characteristics of an ideal student leader center on strong communication and social skills conveyed in an empathetic and encouraging manner. This type of social interaction style serves as a model to group members of how to appropriately engage and behave together (Kouzes & Posner, 2002). Group members must feel that their personal disclosures and their individuality are respected and validated by both the leaders and fellow group members. Student leaders accomplish this respect and validation by expressing nonjudgment, empathy, and understanding throughout the group meeting. Enthusiasm, motivation, and praise of group members are helpful, but not enough to foster the richness of group connection and cohesion. Rather, student leaders must recognize and monitor the delicate balance between their roles as an authority within the group while simultaneously being part of the group itself. This dual role is demonstrated by fluidly switching among offering feedback, offering instruction, and sharing appropriate personal self-reflection and disclosures.

Students' Responsibilities as Peer Leaders

The student leader shares a number of responsibilities when cofacilitating a group discussion with fellow peers. The leaders actively work together to create comfort and encourage disclosure from their group members. They also proactively display appropriate and positive behavior toward each other and group members. Because group conflict and tension are a normative and expected part of group dynamics (Tuckman & Jensen, 1977), leaders are expected to intervene assertively in a nonjudgmental and empathic manner to reduce group fragmentation and dysfunction. In addition, peer leaders demonstrate tolerance and patience when ambiguity and intense emotions are presented by validating and normalizing these experiences as part of the group experience. The priority for the leaders is on the process and dynamic of the group rather than content, and experienced leaders recognize that the content provides a context in which the group members can all connect. Ultimately, the peer leaders develop a rhythm and collaborative dynamic based on competing influences of structure and flexibility as dictated by the needs of each group member and their evolving roles and experiences from meeting to meeting. One marker of leader effectiveness manifests itself when the group begins to operate in a self-sufficient and active manner without direct facilitation from the leaders.

Selection of Leaders

At the higher education institutional level, selecting leaders among students is often a collaboration between multiple offices to identify and select students for a variety of leadership positions across campus. For example, faculty members, student life staff, and other university administrative offices may help to identify those who would be ideal in specific peer-based leadership roles. Typically, the selection process involves at least three primary steps: recruitment, application, and interview.

Recruiting leaders typically takes place in the spring semester of the academic year before the fall programs commence. Notices posted in buildings across campus and sent electronically to the student body invite interested students to apply. Current student leaders and other related resources, including faculty and student life staff, are requested to give recommendations for students who they believe would be competent future leaders.

Interested students are then asked to complete an application and submit it to the faculty or program directors. The application includes relevant questions briefly assessing the student's qualifications, such as academic record, previous and current experience in other leadership roles, and plans for the future.

Following a recruitment period of two weeks, the faculty or program directors review the applications and select the most qualified students for an interview. During the interview, students are asked to describe their background and leadership experiences that they feel would prepare them to colead a group of their peers. The Faculty Program Directors give an overview of the leadership responsibilities including expectations for group meetings and training and supervision during the program. After the interviews, the most qualified students are invited to begin peer leadership training.

CHAPTER 4

Training Students to Lead

Preliminary Leadership Training Workshops

An initial training session or organized seminar is essential to help prepare novice student leaders for the experience of facilitating a group discussion of peers. A common approach to training is to develop and implement a workshop focused on the topic at hand. This approach is used across disciplines such as science, business, and health to educate participants with the basic knowledge and skillset needed to begin the experience (Allan, Bland, & Dawson, 1990; Gosser & Roth, 1998). Research indicates workshop participants reported an increase in confidence, knowledge, and technical skills following the workshop (Pandey et al., 2005). In addition, evidence suggests that continuing education seminars and other educational workshops are associated with positive outcomes in professional practice (Thomason O'Brien et al., 2001).

A number of essential elements must be included in an effective workshop (de Grave, Zanting, Mansvelder-Longayroux, & Molenaar, 2014; Steinert, 2009). For an effective workshop, the facilitators must be familiar with the needs of the audience and consider the specific learning objectives they hope the audience will achieve as a result of the workshop. Facilitators select specific learning activities and other educational resources to enhance the learning experience, such as problem-solving (Sork, 1984). With this in mind, we designed the workshops outlined below specifically for the advanced undergraduate student preparing to serve as a peer leader to other students in their social community. In particular, students who participate in these workshops receive an introduction to leading a peer-based program.

The T2U program will be used as an illustration of a peer-based program for designing and implementing student leadership training workshops.

Workshop 1: Introductory Training for Leaders in the T2U Program

At the beginning of the academic term before the leaders have met with their peer groups for the first time, a two- to three-hour training session introduces the leaders to the basic structure of the program and rudimentary skills in group facilitation. This training session also gives the leaders an opportunity to meet and begin to establish collegial relationships. Ideally, training on more specific skills and topics will continue for the students weekly throughout the duration of the program (Harper & Allegretti, 2015). In the first workshop, a lecture-based approach with visual aids outlining the basics of the program serves as the premise for the workshop with opportunities to engage in interactive, problem-solving tasks embedded throughout (Sork, 1984). The following points provide a general outline of the introductory training workshop with examples from a program focused on assisting first-year students with the transition to college (the T2U program):

The Purpose of the Program

The purpose of this program is to help first-year students with their transition and adjustment to higher education and university life. In addition, this program serves as an opportunity to develop new friendships and social connections within a small-group setting.

The History of the Program

The T2U program has been implemented across a variety of higher education institutions ranging from small, private liberal arts colleges to large, public universities, including Queens University of Charlotte and Wilfred Laurier University. The program was adapted and revised from a manual to fit the needs of the specific institution (Hunsberger, Pancer, Pratt, Rog, & Alisat, 2003).

The Format of the Sessions

Each group session follows the same format beginning with a check-in with each group member, a focused discussion on a topic relevant to the first-year students' transition, and then exercises or activities to promote problem-solving and strategies for dealing with normative transition issues. The sessions end with a written evaluation of the session and a wrap-up and introduction of the topic for the following week. Although each session follows this format, time afforded to each section of the session will change over the course of the semester. For instance, the check-in may be relatively brief when the groups initially meet; however, as students become more comfortable and familiar with each other, this portion of the session may take longer.

The Topics and Dates for the Sessions

An overview of the topics for the semester and the schedule for the topics are provided for review. For example, Session 2 in the T2U program focuses on forming new social connections on campus and encouraging first-year students to participate in on-campus organized activities.

The Role of the Leaders

Student leaders in the group sessions strive to provide an opportunity for first-year students to discuss experiences that occur during their first year on campus. The leaders will use the group facilitation skills that they learn and that are reinforced in their weekly training course to promote an open and inclusive discussion of the topic. As part of their role, the leaders will provide support for the group members and act as models for the other members of the group. At all times, the peer leaders must ensure that the members of the group understand the ethical guidelines and must remind group members of these guidelines throughout the semester. In addition, leaders work together in teams to co-lead their peer group.

Training for First Meeting (Session 1)

During this initial training session, the leaders will review step-by-step what they will do in Session 1 of their peer support group. They will also have the opportunity to practice parts of it with the other leaders before they meet with their own groups. Practice exercises include introductions and other "icebreaker" activities. During Session 1, the leaders will begin to establish the atmosphere of the group as being warm and inclusive. They should prepare the materials needed before the peer group's first meeting. These materials may include snacks, drinks, handouts (e.g., outline of sessions, guidelines, rationale for the groups), pencils, evaluation forms, and attendance forms.

Activity #1: Role Play Introductions

At this point in the training session, the student leaders practice the "dual interview icebreaker" that is used in the first peer group meeting (Session 1) by role-playing the interviews with their coleaders. This exercise also serves as an opportunity for the coleaders to get to know one another better and begin to establish and develop their coleader relationship. The student leaders should spend five to ten minutes asking each other questions about their background, family, interests, or other points of interest. When all of the student leaders have finished talking to their partners, the pairs will introduce each other to the rest of the group with details about their lives that they found interesting.

Review of Program

In this section of the introductory training workshop, the student leaders will review important aspects of the program that will be discussed with the new group in Session 1. The topics listed below are examples of important aspects of the program:

1. The rationale of the program
2. The guidelines of the program
3. The schedule and topics of discussion for the semester
4. The focused discussion topic for Session 1

Activity #2: Role Play Focused Discussion

At this point in the training, the student leaders will practice leading a discussion on the expectations about university life. Leaders volunteer to play different roles (e.g., well-adjusted student, homesick student, disengaged student).

Evaluation

Student leaders will discuss important assessment measures taken throughout the program, including both weekly evaluations of the session and the leaders and attendance.

Discussion #1: Challenges

After going through the outline of Session 1, the training workshop now focuses on the challenges student leaders might face among group members. In this problem-solving exercise, student leaders generate solutions in which to deal with them. Examples of challenges include:

1. What do you do if one student dominates the group?
2. What do you do if someone repeatedly interrupts other group members?
3. What do you do if a group member does not participate?
4. What do you do if you find out that group member has violated confidentiality?
5. What do you do if a group member leaves the room crying?
6. What do you do if one of the group members gets angry and verbally abusive toward another member?
7. What do you do if a group member violates the group guidelines for cell phone use and repeatedly texts during the group meeting?

Activity #3: Role Play a Challenging Situation

At this point in the training, the leaders will practice how to handle some of these situations with the leaders volunteering to play the roles of the peer group members and the leader. The group may then discuss various options that the leaders offer for resolving the situation.

Wrap-up

At the end of the first training workshop, the leaders should share their concerns and review solutions.

Workshop 2: Empowerment and Diversity Training

Following the first workshop, additional workshops on specific topics may be introduced throughout the semester. These workshops are in addition to the weekly training and supervisory sessions that occur in the regular classroom setting. They provide emphasis on an issue that is significant to the student population of the institution. One such topic is empowering a diverse student population. The following workshop gives an example of how to introduce working with a diverse population of students and how to empower students to overcome obstacles that may impede their successful transition. In this workshop, leaders explore feelings of self-determination, meaning, and competence, and investigate how to apply these concepts to personal and professional relationships. Using these concepts, the leaders facilitate discussions of diversity issues with the members of their groups. These discussions may be informally related to different topics or deliberately interwoven into the discussion topics over the semester. The workshop also provides another context in which the student leaders may gain insight into the beliefs that they hold. In this example, the workshop is divided into three one-hour sessions that may be held on the same day or may be held as distinct sessions on separate occasions.

The goal of this workshop is to increase knowledge and skills of leaders working with diverse populations of students. Prior to the workshop, leaders are asked to read literature relevant to the topic at hand. Specifically, leaders read the book *Citizen* by Claudia Rankin (2014). This reading serves as a foundational and informative context, and its related themes are interwoven throughout the workshop series. As a preliminary assignment, leaders are asked to select one or two passages from the book that inspired or engaged them.

Session 1

In Session 1, the workshop begins with an interactive activity designed to socially engage the leaders. Specifically, leaders are invited to share personal aspects or characteristics of themselves with each other. This exercise is followed by an open discussion about forming new relationships followed by additional activities to prepare them for Session 2.

Activity #1: Get to Know Your Coleader

Leaders may respond to the following question: If you could ask just one question to discover a person's suitability for _____ (e.g., Roommate/Friend/Romantic Partner/Coleader), what would your question be? Why is this information important to you to know about a person?

Activity #2: Large-Group Discussion: New Relationships

For the second activity, leaders may respond to the following questions:

1. What process do people go through when looking for new relationships?
2. What characteristic is important to you when establishing a new relationship and why is that characteristic important to you?
3. How would you see that characteristic in yourself and in others, even in your T2U group?
4. What common characteristics/themes did you hear across the group?
5. Was there ever an instance when someone recognized a characteristic in you that you may not have realized was important? What was it? Why do you imagine it was important to them?

Activity #3: Empowerment Strategies

Leaders are encouraged to brainstorm strategies that promote positivity, confidence, and empowerment. Examples of these strategies may range from physical activity such as exercise and other body movements to cognitive- and emotional-based strategies such as developing mantras of self-affirmation, engaging in mindfulness or meditation practices, or expressing gratitude toward others.

Session 2

Session 2 facilitates critical thinking skills among the leaders about concepts and experiences students of diverse backgrounds may experience. First, leaders will participate in an interactive activity about classification of others and the associated connotations of criticism and bias or stereotypes. Second, leaders will discuss the passages and inherent themes of a related nature from the book *Citizen* (Rankin, 2014).

Activity #1: Classification Game

In this activity, the workshop facilitators should:

1. Explain the concept of "pigeonholing" someone and discuss how this classification is based on stereotyping that is typically judgmental and unhelpful.
2. Divide the group into smaller groups of four or five people and ask them to discuss their personal likes and dislikes. For example, participants may learn that they are all "night owls" or prefer pizza over other types of food.
3. Ask the groups to identify subgroups of people with similar interests that are neutral and do not hold any negative stereotypes, such as groups with similar musical interests.

Discussion #1: Identity

This discussion is designed to give student leaders the opportunity to explore their identity. In this discussion, the leaders should answer the following questions:

1. How did you identify yourselves?
2. Do you still feel that "label" accurately defines who you are? What are the associated stereotypes of just one label?
3. Have you been "pigeonholed"? Have you "pigeonholed" others?

Activity #2: Small-Group Brainstorming for Discussion Questions for *Citizen*

In this activity, the leaders should discuss the following questions:

1. What did you like or not like about the book?
2. What was your favorite passage?
3. What was most meaningful to you about the book?
4. What surprised you?
5. Did you find any of the passages chilling?

Session 3

In this final session of the workshop on empowerment and diversity, leaders will apply what they have read and discussed to their own peer support groups. The session begins with a discussion about the book *Citizen* followed by an interactive brainstorming experience to create related scenarios and activities to lead within their own peer group.

Discussion #1: *Citizen* Discussion

1. In this discussion, the student leaders will discuss one or two of their favorite passages from the book and explain what happened and their reaction.
2. Following this discussion, the leaders should participate in a brainstorming session in which they consider what they would do if they found themselves in that situation. For example, if student leaders witnessed one of the scenarios described in the book passage, how would they respond, if at all?
3. After generating examples from the book that were meaningful and memorable, the leaders should suggest how they would present the example to their own peer group.

Activity #1: Writing Scenarios for the Peer Groups

In this activity, the student leaders will have the opportunity to apply what they have learned about diversity to their peer group of first-year students. This activity includes the following:

1. In small groups, the leaders should discuss themes and examples in *Citizen*.
2. The leaders should create a diversity session with a scenario and activity that they could use with their first-year student group. For instance, student leaders may choose an example of a micro aggression and write a scenario describing it. Then they would ask the first-year students what they would do in that situation.
3. All of the student leaders should share and discuss with each other their scenarios.

Workshop 3: First-Generation Students' Training

The goal of this workshop is to increase leaders' knowledge and understanding of first-generation students and to learn the best methods of empowering these students to succeed in higher education.

Session 1

In Session 1, the workshop begins with an interactive, problem-solving activity designed to engage the leaders. This is followed by an open discussion of the topic followed by additional activities to prepare them for Session 2.

Activity #1: What Will Open this Door?

This activity is designed to help student leaders experience what it feels like to be naïve or unable to solve a problem when it is clear others know the solution. This experience may be quite similar to what first-generation students experience when entering college. This activity includes the following:

1. Begin by asking the leaders to consider a picture of a door and be prepared to solve the following problem: What is the key that will open this door for you?

2. Immediately offer examples of solutions for what will open the door. For instance, the key for opening the door could be words with a particular letter in them. Offer only the examples but do not offer the rule embedded in generating the correct answer.

3. After giving five or six examples, the workshop facilitators should ask the leaders who figured out the key to opening the door to raise their hands. Do not tell the key.

4. These leaders should add their own creative solutions to the words that will open the door. Their solutions should indicate that they have clearly identified the key (or rule).

5. After a number of leaders have participated, the workshop facilitators should ask the leaders to reveal the key.

6. The workshop facilitators should ask the leaders who did not figure out the key to open the door to describe what it felt like to be unable to solve the problem. Specifically, the leaders may share their thoughts and feelings about the moment when they realized their peers knew the key and they did not.

7. The leaders should then describe what it felt like for them to go to an institution of higher education for the first time.

8. The workshop facilitators should ask the leaders to imagine how a first-generation student may feel about attending an institution of higher education.

9. The workshop facilitators should conclude the activity with basic information about first-generation students. For example, they may describe how many institutions or higher education are reaching out to underserved populations including first-generation students. They may also include information about the steps that their own institution is taking to be more inclusive.

Activity #2: Writing about Your First Experiences on Campus

This activity may take place in the workshop or may be given as a take-home assignment. The writing assignment is designed to engage the leaders by reviewing their own experience as first-year students on campus. The student leaders should respond to the following prompt:

Please share your own experiences as a college student and what resources you may have used to support your transition to college. This could be personal support through family experience or by using academic/institutional supports here on campus. When writing your narrative, please reflect on your family's background and experience, especially as it relates to higher education. When you were preparing to come here, who gave you support/information? When you arrived on campus, what was your support like? To whom did you go? Which services did you use on campus, if any? Please expect to discuss your narrative (if you feel comfortable sharing it with the group) and others' narratives.

Session 2

Session 2 in the workshop series focuses on connecting the leaders' own experiences as a first-year student with those commonly experienced by first-generation students. Similar to Session 1, this session includes both discussion and activities designed to engage the student leader in an interactive learning experience.

Discussion #1: Large-Group Discussion about Personal Narratives

This discussion gives the student leaders an opportunity to describe their personal narratives about attending college. The workshop facilitators should ask the student leaders if they would like to share their personal narratives. Then they should ask the leaders the following:

1. Identify characteristics from the personal narratives of those who described themselves as first-generation students (e.g., persistent, independent, competent).
2. Compare and contrast the characteristics of students who are and who are not first generation.
3. Describe how those characteristics would help a first-year student to give examples of identity that they heard in the narratives. Ask them how they identified themselves.

4. Discuss whether they still feel that "label" that they had for them-selves when they entered college still accurately defines them and the associated stereotypes of having just one label.

The discussion should conclude with the student leaders identifying examples from their peer groups of students being "pigeon-holed."

Activity #1: Brainstorming Session

For this activity, leaders should reflect on the personal narratives just shared in a large-group discussion. Prompts for discussion include the following:

1. What was most meaningful or what surprised them about each oth-er's personal narratives?
2. Which narratives may be meaningful or relevant to first-year students?
3. How would you present these ideas to first-year students?

Session 3

The goal of this final session in the workshop series is to challenge leaders to apply what they have heard and learned into strategic activities to use with their own peer groups. As before, this workshop session emphasizes interactive problem-solving, critical thinking skills, and active discussion to maintain engagement and interest of the student leaders.

Activity #1: Locks and Keys

Leaders should generate examples of "locked doors" that are potential obstacles to success for a first-year student. They should then develop strategies, "keys," for the first-year students to "unlock the door." For instance, a "locked door" might happen during registration when first-year students may not get into a class that they need. The "key" might be to have additional classes to choose from as substitutes for their initial choice. Another "locked door" may be that first-year students do not understand the material in a class and they are afraid that they will fail an upcoming test. A successful key to unlock this door may include setting up a meeting with the professor or making an appointment at a campus resource like a tutoring center.

Activity #2: Application of the Personal Narratives

In this activity, leaders should review their small-group brainstorming experience in Session 2 of the workshop series. They should then work in small groups to create activities or scenarios that illustrate meaningful concepts discussed from their personal narratives. This activity includes the following:

1. Student leaders should be divided into small groups.
2. Student leaders should use the personal narratives of the first-generation students to create a list of themes, characteristics, or principles that they described.
3. Student leaders should develop a scenario or activity to use with their peer groups that illustrate these concepts.
4. Student leaders should identify how the scenarios could be used in their own peer groups.

CHAPTER 5

Coleading Groups

Using two or more facilitators instead of an individual leader is generally understood and widely accepted in both the professional and empirical literature to offer multiple advantages and enhanced outcomes for both leaders and group members (Lundin & Aronov, 1952; Kivlighan, London, & Miles, 2011; Yalom & Leszcz, 2005). The advantages of coleaders include two voices of reason and perspectives which can be at times similar, and even more importantly different or competing, thus providing opportunities for healthy discourse and negotiation. In addition, coleaders in a group setting may offer a mature example of healthy relational dynamics within a dyad (Vannicelli, 1992; Yalom & Leszcz, 2005). Group members benefit from two leaders as indicated by increased group member participation, higher group satisfaction, and higher overall group effectiveness (Kivlighan, London, & Miles, 2011). Given that coleadership is the preferred format for group interventions, dyadic leadership teams comprised of mixed gender are not uncommon. Gender has been found to play a pivotal role in influencing group dynamics, including equalizing gender roles in stereotypes and resocialization, working through gender distortion, and modeling healthy female–male interaction based on mutual respect, gender equality, and role flexibility (Garvin & Reed, 1983; Kahn, 1996; Paulson, Burroughs, & Gelb, 1976; Moreno, Kramer, Scheidegger, & Weitzman, 2005; Nosko & Wallace, 1997).

Building the Coleader Relationship

Coleadership is defined as the process of leading a group or team in collaboration with another with the goal of facilitating a productive outcome for its group members (Corey & Corey, 2003; Gladding, 2003;

Yalom, 1995). Building the coleader relationship depends upon a number of factors, including whether or not one leader is more experienced than the other, their history of working together, and their allotting adequate time to build and develop their relational dynamic.

A number of theories on the coleader relationship have focused primarily on concepts that illustrate the dynamic between the two leaders. These concepts range from negotiation of status within the group to competency and trust issues (Atieno Okech & Kline, 2006; Berger, 2002). Research indicates the coleader relationship is impacted when coleaders evaluate themselves as less knowledgeable or capable when compared to their coleader (Berger, 2002; Cohen & DeLois, 2001). Such a self-evaluation can negatively impact the coleaders' ability to lead and implement skills effectively (Yalom & Leszcz, 2005). In fact, the coleader relationship is often compared to and associated with the dynamic factors found between married and other intimate dyadic couples. These factors include communication issues, power struggles, and intimacy (Luke & Hackey, 2007). However, the attention to these elements of this collaborative relationship fails to fully convey the developmental and maturing process of the coleader pair.

Early efforts to conceptualize this process initially emphasized intrapsychic and interpersonal elements of the coleader relationship that evolve through a series of stages within a therapeutic framework (Dick, Lessler, & Whiteside, 1980). More recently, Fall and Wejnert (2005) incorporated previous theories by applying Tuckman and Jensen's (1977) classic five-stage model of group development to the congruent development of the coleader relationship. This approach streamlined the understanding of the coleaders' developmental process by embedding it within a recognized, and well-accepted, model of group development (Burn, 2004; Johnson & Johnson, 2013). In addition, this perspective suggests the evolution of the coleader relationship is integrated within the same process and conditions as the entire group's developing dynamic (Fall & Wejnert, 2005).

Similar to the beginning of the development of the group, the coleader relationship begins with the Forming stage. Fall and Wejnert (2005) suggested that the coleaders are normatively struggling to find their place as a leader within the group and with each other. Anxiety and confusion are common for even seasoned coleaders in the early stages of their group dynamic, and they may display those feelings by engaging in overly active ways of connecting with the group such as tandeming. Tandeming occurs when coleaders engage in excessive verbalization in an attempt to assert their authority and connect with the group (Gallogly & Levine, 1979). For example, one leader may offer feedback and advice to a group member, and the coleader may immediately interject a similar comment before the group member has a chance to respond or reflect. This interaction may inadvertently reduce the impact of the leaders' feedback if it is too repetitive and offered prematurely from both coleaders. In addition, tandeming can even lead group members to misinterpret a competitive power struggle between coleaders.

As comfort within the group begins to increase, coleaders may find themselves transitioning into the Storming stage. Demonstrations of this stage include more displays of confidence and disclosure of personal aspects from each leader. For example, one coleader may feel more comfortable disclosing a specific, yet personal, interpretation or opinion that provides a more personal insight that is shared with the group members and the coleader. Taking these risks helps to facilitate the shedding of the "façade" or social "politeness" and brings authenticity and genuineness into the group and coleader dynamics. Coleaders should anticipate, and even hope for, normative dyadic conflict as each leader begins to take risks and make assertions that expose their differences in personality styles and leadership techniques. These differences predictably activate feelings of adequacy and self-assessment, and coleaders who are able to process and communicate their thoughts and feelings about these emerging differences can assist each other and the group with progressing to the third stage, Norming. Failure to do so can lead both the coleaders and group to remain stagnant and paralyzed in power struggles or constant renegotiation of power and possibly even to regress into shallow and insignificant interactions reminiscent of the Forming stage.

Following successful resolution of the Storming stage, the coleaders' relationship in the Norming stage becomes much more cohesive and connected than before. This connection may be indicated by a sense of ownership and shared responsibility in addition to feelings of comfort and the support of having a genuine partner within the group. In addition, evidence suggests that coleaders will experience a decrease in preoccupation with competency concerns as openness and trust continue to build between coleaders (Atieno Okech & Kline, 2006). Fall and Wejnert (2005) cautioned coleaders to stay mindful of collusion, whereby coleaders may be hesitant to fully disclose perspectives for fear of any differences between coleaders disrupting the newly experienced alignment and balanced state of the relationship and group. However, empirical evidence indicates dissimilarity between coleaders, especially as it relates to leadership styles and skills, has been associated with a more productive group climate (Miles & Kivlighan, 2008) and positive group member outcomes (Piper, Doan, Edwards, & Jones, 1979). Characteristics of dissimilarity between coleaders can be expanded even further to include the positive impact of differences in coleaders' physical appearance and personality styles on client outcomes (Dick, Lessler, & Whiteside, 1980). In a recent study, Miles and Kivlighan (2010) found coleader dissimilarity was associated with higher levels of engagement and conflict within the group. The increased conflict was found to be a positive outcome given the context and sample assessed; specifically, the researchers brought together social groups that historically experience tension for intergroup dialogue. Thus, their finding of increased conflict associated with coleader dissimilarity was a desirable and positive association.

As the coleaders progress further in their relationship, the Performing stage offers one of the most exciting and empowering stages of group and coleader development. A key indicator of this stage is the group's fluidity and independence of functioning separate and apart from the coleaders' direction. Group leaders may observe their own decrease in overt verbal direction and instruction as the group begins to take ownership and moves together as a cohesive unit. In contrast, coleaders may fully embrace a more facilitative role by subtly steering and guiding the group's discussion, and, in some way, they may appear to be more part of the group rather than leading it. Fall and Wejnert (2005) recommended leaders at this point engage in techniques that promote open and direct communication as a whole. One technique they suggested is forecasting. Forecasting occurs when a leader takes the initiative to confidently assert the direction of conversation the group will move in together. For example, a leader may say to the group, "With that story in mind, I think this is an opportunity for us to discuss the issue of how we experience conflict and distress, as it appears this is a topic that is resonating with all of us here." A second technique would be process observation. With this technique, leaders openly share their internal thoughts and feelings about what is going on with the group. For example, a leader may comment to the entire group, "I am sensing a bit of frustration and irritability in the room, and I wonder if others are experiencing that as well." These techniques demonstrate the group's closeness, maturity, and ability to handle "live" processing within the group. Through role modeling, leaders exemplify behaviors or ways for the group to engage in on their own discussion, thereby furthering enhancing the independence of the group.

As the group draws to an end, the coleader relationship enters into the Adjourning stage. For both the group and the coleaders, this stage brings a range of fluctuating emotions and thoughts around termination. Fall and Wejnert (2005) advised coleaders to be mindful of the re-emergence of previously resolved behaviors and other regressive issues, such as collusion and power struggles. Rather, the coleaders again model and emulate an appropriate and healthy resolution to an intimate experience. The coleaders should assess when termination is most appropriate to occur and begin to adequately prepare within that time line. Coleaders may even devise a ritual or shared activity that clearly summarizes and processes the overall experience and then ultimately brings it to a close.

Suggested Activities to Build the Coleader Relationship

There are a number of essential activities coleaders should engage in to ensure the success of their collaboration and facilitation of their group exits. These activities are instrumental in assisting coleaders to overcome potential obstacles during their group experience. They may be implemented based on the appropriate timing and stage of the group; however, revisiting these activities is encouraged throughout the group process.

In the Planning phase, coleaders are encouraged to sit down one-on-one and get to know each other (e.g., "coleader date"). In addition to sharing relevant details about each other, this preparatory exercise provides opportunity to establish common orientation and understanding about the goals and expectations of the group experience. Coleaders may review the guidelines for the group with each other and preemptively agree on early identification and handling of potential problems that may disrupt the group. Coleaders may also agree upon initial roles and responsibilities in the group (Paulson, Burroughs, & Gelb, 1976).

In the Working phase of coleading a group, coleaders are encouraged to strengthen their relationship by engaging regularly in debriefing meetings after each group meeting. This debriefing provides an ongoing conversation of feedback and reflection whereby coleaders can more openly express opinions and feelings related to the group process without the presence of the group members. Coleaders should review the session content and group dynamic and also evaluate together each leader's contribution to the group discussion. As normative group process issues begin to arise, revisions of coleaders' roles and suggestions for managing specific group processes can be proposed and discussed privately. Moreover, regular supervision with a trained facilitator can assist coleaders with a more profound understanding of the nuances of the group process coupled with the coleader dynamic. The supervisor serves as the coach or consultant of the group experience and can offer instruction and guidance on the inner processes and dynamics between leaders and group members. In addition, should conflict emerge between the coleaders themselves, the supervisor serves as a mediator and facilitates conflict negotiation and resolution.

In the Concluding phase of coleading a group, coleaders no longer rely upon activities such as supervision for guidance and debriefing. Quite possibly, coleaders may even require less intense, prescribed activities with each other now that the group is fluidly functioning as a cohesive entity. In fact, coleaders may find the group is connected enough for processing to occur within the group itself. Instead, activities during this phase that may be most appropriate would be periodic preparatory and/or debriefing meetings, to ensure both coleaders' ideas are consistent with respect to outcome goals for the group.

CHAPTER 6

Group Facilitation Techniques

Nonverbal and verbal communication are two basic categories of group facilitation techniques and are areas in which leaders may concentrate on building their skills and understanding. Student leaders must be aware of the interplay between these two types of communication styles and elect to assert one or both types in a meaningful manner. Asserting these techniques depends upon a myriad of factors, including the leaders' confidence and ability to display the technique and also the intended outcome of the demonstrated communication.

Nonverbal Communication Techniques

Between 60 and 70 percent of understanding and meaning in interpersonal communication derives from nonverbal behavior (Moore, Hickson, & Stacks, 2013). When one group member is speaking, all the other members are communicating nonverbally as well. Examples of these nonverbal behaviors include facial expressions, body posture, and body orientation. For example, level of interest may be communicated by the leaders' body position. They may face either away with their arms and legs folded or toward the speaker with their body open in a relaxed manner. Facial expressions include smiling, looking away, pursed lips, raised eyebrows, and eye contact. These subtle messages of communication offer clues about the group members' internal states. A proficient leader continually scans the room, occasionally breaking eye contact with the speaking group member to check in with the nonverbal cues from the rest of the group. This effective method of leadership models for group members that the leaders include the group as a whole and expect the group to be included in the discussion as well.

Listening as a Technique

Listening is an effective nonverbal leadership tool that promotes engagement and connection. Whitworth, Kimsey-House, Kimsey-House, and Sandahl (2007) identified multiple levels of listening. For example, a group member may share a personal narrative, and the student leaders initially attend to the content as it relates specifically to that person. Over time, however, student leaders may begin to take a single personal narrative and extrapolate themes or topics that indirectly address or relate to the group as a whole. They become adept at deciphering and expanding upon the emotive and intuitive depth, or themes, within the content itself. As proficiency with listening as a technique improves, student leaders may engage in various types of listening, such as discriminative or analytical listening (Engleberg & Wynn, 2013). When using discriminative listening, student leaders critically identify and evaluate what information is important. In contrast, when using analytical listening, student leaders determine how the information relates to the group as a whole and use this information in a meaningful way.

Silence as a Technique

Silence operates to indicate attentive and engaged listening. According to Kurzon (2007), silence serves multiple functions in group discussions ranging from connection and binding (e.g., "let's take a moment to think about what he just said") to revelational (e.g., "Wow, what a story. I'm not sure what to say other than how much I appreciate your sharing. I would like to take a moment to process it all"). Novice student leaders may feel compelled to fill the space with words quickly; in fact, lengthy silences may inadvertently create undue anxiety within the group if the group is within the initial stages of development and cohesion (e.g., Forming; Tuckman, 1965; Tuckman & Jensen, 1977). However, in more established groups, silences among group members allow the group to connect with each other and the process while also inviting group members to consider what to say and how to respond (Knapp, 2007; Ladany, Hill, Thompson, & O'Brien, 2004).

As leaders gain comfort with silence over time, they can begin to evaluate whether silence is constructive or destructive. In a constructive way, silence illustrates tolerance and acceptance of the present moment and anticipation and interest of further responses and information that is about to come (Levitt, 2001). For example, a leader may comment to the group, "I'm aware of how quiet it is; who would like to share what is going on for them right now?" Leaders who appear attentive via eye contact, head nodding, and smiling allow group members the space and time to self-reflect, organize, and articulate their inner thoughts and feelings. In addition, silence serves as a positive challenge by encouraging group members to take healthy and safe risks. For example, silence can be interpreted as an invitation to further self-disclose (Duba, 2004). In a destructive way, silence among group members who do not share or participate regularly may be perceived by others in the group as judgmental, critical, and possibly passively hostile. Group members may struggle to connect with these fellow members when such limited information and interaction is offered. In these situations, leaders must be attuned to how potentially damaging the silence is to the rest of the group and assess whether or not an appropriate intervention is warranted to assist the group as a whole. For example, a leader may direct a nonjudgmental and inviting question to the quiet group member such as, "I noticed how quiet you were today. I'm curious what was going on for you. Would you be willing to share just a bit about how you are doing?" Student leaders can anticipate the quiet group member may not share an elaborative verbal response; however, even in this exchange, the student leaders demonstrate to the group that silence can be informative and that the quiet group member is still engaged and connected to the group.

Verbal Communication Techniques

The words leaders choose to say during a group process experience play an integral role in leading and connecting the group. Using words such as we, us, and our can quickly and efficiently facilitate a sense of cohesion and bonding. The impact and effectiveness of verbal language among the group is even more enhanced by the proxemics of the group (Hall, 1982). The social use of physical space, especially personal space, plays a critical role in the quality of discussion and cohesion of the group (Hall, 1982). Leaders should organize the room and seating in a way that invites open dialogue, productive interaction, and shared investment in the group experience. Early on, leaders should begin to identify and draw attention to patterns or themes that resonate and connect group members. Leaders may point out these patterns of themes by verbalizing observable behaviors (e.g., "I noticed you seemed to have a reaction to what was said when you shifted in your seat."), offering clarifying responses (e.g., "Let me see if I can summarize what you are saying to be sure I truly understand you."), or inviting self-disclosure (e.g., "Would you please share more about your personal experience?").

Self-Disclosure as a Technique

Self-disclosure is an essential part of joining and connecting with a group, and as such, it is imperative that student leaders gain confidence and skill with inviting self-disclosure among their group members. An effective and useful tool to encourage self-disclosure is through social modeling, whereby leaders share their own personal experiences related to the discussion topics. Careful consideration in using self-disclosure as a technique is necessary because the leaders need to balance relatedness with their group members while also maintaining an authoritative presence. Upon self-disclosing, student leaders must be astute in recognizing subtle cues from group members indicating they may want to share something in response but may be hesitant to do so. Calling directly upon group members in a relaxed and supportive manner can increase confidence and appreciation of being recognized. For example, some group members may be too shy to speak up independently; however, they may willingly take the invitation to do so if asked directly.

Validating versus Invalidating Verbal Techniques

Leaders may rely on a variety of verbal techniques to facilitate group discussion and ultimately cohesion. These may be categorized into either validating or invalidating responses that impact the overall group. Validating comments are ones that affirm and support the group member(s) and encourage participation and connection. The following are examples of suggested validating communication techniques:

1. ***Immediate recognition.*** One of the primary ways leaders can effectively and efficiently validate a group member is by directly acknowledging the group member's statement. An example of this immediate recognition is to respond, "That is a very honest and open statement; thank you for sharing with the group."

2. ***Checking assumptions.*** Leaders always strive to bring the assumptions people are operating under out into the open, so they can be clarified, corrected, and clearly understood by everyone. An assumption is something taken for granted or presupposed, typically based upon previous learning and part of one's personal belief system. An example of checking an assumption is to say, "I'm curious about your beliefs about this personal topic. Would you mind sharing with us about how this belief came to be? Is this something you learned from your family? Do you find it remains accurate for yourself based on your experiences?"

3. ***Empathy.*** Expressing empathy is an essential part of communication. Empathy conveys to the other person that his or her perspective and emotions are understood and regarded with respect and acceptance. It is fundamentally different from sympathy, although the two are commonly, yet erroneously, mistaken for each other. While sympathy is an expression of distress, sorrow, or pity for the other person's misfortune or difficulty, empathy is characterized by accurately verbalizing and displaying feelings that indicate the listener is truly "in the shoes" of the other person. An example of expressing empathy is saying, "I can only imagine how you must have felt during that event. If that had happened to me, I would have felt very similarly to what you have described. The experience must have felt overwhelming."

4. ***Paraphrasing.*** Leaders summarize, or paraphrase, consistently during group discussions. Paraphrasing illustrates to the group members that leaders are not only listening, but they are also oriented in the same direction as the speaker or group. Paraphrasing can take the

form of repeating specifically what has been said, or it may go a step further by offering a summary of one's understanding of what has been said. It allows others to hear their points again and opens the door to clarification of key points. An example of paraphrasing is to say, "So let me make sure I understand what you are saying."

5. *Inspiring.* Leaders actively engage the group and add energy, comments, and feedback in a way that enlivens the group, encourages participation, and maintains movement toward progress and the group's goals. An example of inspiring is to reply, "Wow, I am so inspired today by what has been shared! It makes me think of our goals we identified several meetings ago and how far our group has come during our time together."

6. *Harmonizing.* Leaders can use harmonizing to encourage group cohesion and teamwork. For example, leaders may use humor as a relief or an inclusive statement as a way to synchronize the group, particularly after a difficult discussion. An example of harmonizing is the statement that, "It is so unexpected and exciting to realize each and every one of us has experienced this event at some point already. Who would have thought we had so much in common given how different we all initially seemed to be? There are so many solutions out there that we can share with each other and learn together."

7. *Enhancing the conversation.* Student leaders may elect to add to the conversation by sharing information that reinforces what the member has shared. For example, a statement such as, "I'd like to share a related experience that I believe supports what we just heard" enhances the quality and depth of the conversation while simultaneously validating and supporting the member's experience.

8. *Positive reinforcement.* Leaders who are able to immediately affirm and validate each group member increase the likelihood that the group members will continue to share. An example of a positive reinforcing statement is commenting, "I like your idea" or "That was a very insightful comment."

9. *Elaboration for clarification.* During discussions where leaders and/or group members appear confused or lost with the conversation, the leaders may find it helpful to acknowledge the uncertainty

and invite more elaboration for clarification by asking the following questions:

    a. "I'm not quite sure I understand what you are saying and I want to be sure I do. Would you mind sharing a bit more about this?"

    b. "I believe what you are saying is. . . . (paraphrase); is this correct?"

    c. "Is there anything else about the topic you can share that would relate in some way and give us a better sense of what you mean or are feeling?"

10. ***Checking in.*** Frequently checking in with the group allows for questions and opportunities to process issues such as agenda, time frames, discussion topics, decision methods, and use of information. An example of a check-in would be the statement, "I'd like to revisit the topic that was brought up a few weeks ago to hear if any changes or progress has been made since we last discussed it together."

11. ***Risk taking.*** This technique requires the leader to evaluate the direction and quality of the conversation and consider asserting a related comment or direction. For example, the student leader may say in response to a group member, "I'm not sure how this will be received by the group, but I wanted to share something personal that I think may offer a solution to what we are trying to figure out."

Invalidating techniques are ones that disprove or dismiss the group member(s) and discourage participation and connection. The following are examples of invalidating techniques student leaders are advised to avoid:

1. ***No response.*** Leaders are advised to offer a response that conveys listening or attending to the speaking group member. No response at all unfortunately conveys disinterest, invalidation, avoidance, or dismissal of the group member.

2. ***Circumstantial or peripheral statements.*** At times, leaders may make irrelevant or unnecessary statements within the group. This response may be activated by anxiety or other internal distress related to competency concerns or other leadership issues. For example, leaders may feel compelled to speak often or prematurely

by rambling or telling stories that deviate from the group's discussion. These types of extraneous and digressive statements are inappropriate and potentially damaging to helping the group evolve into a more cohesive unit.

3. ***Dominating.*** Leaders who dominate are those who actively express self-views and opinions for the majority of the time to the disadvantage of the group. In addition, they may try to assert their authority and leadership by monopolizing the time and flow of the group dynamic. Examples of domination include a leader interrupting a group member who is speaking or encouraging the group to move on before the conversation is complete.

4. ***Withdrawing.*** Withdrawal is indicated by leaders removing themselves from discussions or the decision-making process by ignoring what others say or openly refusing to participate. These behaviors negatively impact the group as a whole and invalidate the group process and connection.

5. ***Discounting.*** When leaders disregard or minimize suggested ideas or comments from group members, the group members feel slighted or overlooked. Severe discounting behaviors include insults, which are often in the form of jokes or sarcasm. Leaders need to be mindful of social cues and whether the group may be able to perceive and tolerate sarcasm as humor or whether they would interpret the comments as offensive or rude.

6. ***Blocking.*** Blocking impedes the group progress and cohesion by obstructing ideas and suggestions. A blocking statement that leaders should avoid is saying, "That will never work because . . ." Another example that novice leaders fail to recognize early on as a blocking technique is to say, "Yes, **but** . . ."

7. ***Not taking responsibility.*** Leaders should avoid using the word "you" when sharing feedback to avoid inadvertently creating a climate of defensiveness and caution. Instead, leaders are encouraged to use ownership words such as "I" and "me" to convey responsibility and model to group members how to share their thoughts and feelings with each other. For example, a student leader may say, "I was disappointed and sad to hear about this" instead of "Your comments today made me feel sad and disappointed."

Constructive and Supportive Intervention

At times, leaders will identify necessary opportunities to intervene, whether it is with a specific group member or with the entire group as a whole. The necessity of intervening is predicated upon the outcome goal of group support and cohesion. Interventions may occur when inappropriate or disruptive statements or other dysfunctional behaviors threaten the integrity of the group's cohesion. Alternatively, leaders may elect to intervene to encourage the group's focus to move from one specific topic or member to a wider perspective that impacts the entire group. Over time, and by gaining the trust of the group members and modeling appropriate behaviors, leaders will find that frequent interventions may no longer be needed. As the group's dynamic develops, the members' dependence on facilitation and leadership diminishes in response to their increased engagement and activity with each other.

Deciding whether and when to intervene can be anxiety-producing for any leader, especially in a peer group. The following questions can help determine whether an intervention is needed:

1. Is there an identifiable pattern that continues to emerge among group members?
2. Is there enough trust and respect among the group that the intervention can be appropriately tolerated?
3. What might happen if no intervention were offered? How might the group be impacted by the absence of an intervention?
4. What type of intervention would be offered? What are the risks and rewards of introducing this intervention?
5. Is there enough time to intervene and to also allow the group to process the intervention?

Multiple options for intervention exist, and deciding which intervention to use depends upon the situation, the timing of the situation, the opportunity for intervention, and the intended goal of the intervention. For example, in particular situations, the best choice is for the leaders to intervene directly on behalf of the group, while in another situation, a less direct approach may be more successful. The following are the varying degrees or levels of interventions that may be used to reduce the disruption and re-establish the cohesion of the group:

No Intervention Approach

One approach to consider may be declining to intervene or react at all. For example, it may be best for the leaders to ignore or disregard small demonstrations of inappropriate behaviors or comments from one group member for the benefit of the group as a whole. Drawing attention to these disruptions may in fact have a paradoxical response by reinforcing the behavior and taking further focus and attention from the rest of the group. However, if these behaviors are distracting to the point that the group's process and dynamic become jeopardized and fragmented, it may be best to intervene more directly. In this case, the intervention may also serve as an opportunity for leaders to assertively, yet supportively, demonstrate leadership and authority within the peer group.

Preventive Intervention Approach

One proactive and preventive approach is to set aside a time to explore in advance how group members feel about a specific topic or issue that may be potentially challenging or intimate in nature. Leaders can be better informed and prepared to facilitate discussion about intimate or difficult topics if they have a solid foundation and comprehension of the topic and outline of how the group discussion may go. In addition, leaders can set clear parameters and expectations about behaviors within the group once the group is prepared to engage in the discussion.

Low-Intensity Intervention Approach

The techniques described here are intended to change behavior and the group dynamic in an inclusive and nonconfrontational manner. One approach may be to invite the disruptive group member to share more in an attempt to express interest in truly understanding the group member's thoughts and feelings. Leaders can ask specific and clarifying questions that encourage the group member to elaborate further and paraphrase in an empathetic, yet confident, manner. Once clarification and understanding are secured, the student leaders can offer their own thoughts or feelings in response as a way to model how to engage appropriately in debating discourse. In addition, leaders may invite other group members to ask questions or share their reactions to further explore the situation. Leaders may reframe the topic or situation as a concern that the entire group may want to take on (e.g., "If you found yourself in a similar situation, do you imagine you would think and feel the same way? In a different way? How so?"), or instead elect to discuss how the group dynamic has changed since the disruption occurred (e.g., "I've noticed a slight increase in tension, which is understandable given the topic/feelings/situation. Is anyone else experiencing this tension in our group also?"). Finally, leaders may view this event as an opportunity to remind the group of the guidelines and how disruptions serve as opportunities for connection and growth (e.g., "I know there may be others in the room who feel or think differently and we want to hear those as well. Before we delve further, it's important to remember the guideline of respect and willingness to listen to each other without interruption.").

Medium-Intensity Intervention Approach

Over time, the disruptions may continue to escalate in frequency or intensity, and leaders need to be prepared to introduce a more intentional and significant intervention on behalf of the group. Of course, leaders are encouraged to demonstrate patience and restraint once a low-level intervention is utilized; however, if change does not occur within a reasonable time, leaders have the opportunity to demonstrate more direct leadership skills by implementing a medium-intensity intervention approach to the ongoing situation. One specific technique leaders need to be prepared to use is speaking with the disruptive group member privately either before or after the group. This provides an opportunity for feedback and direct attention, and leaders should not misinterpret this intervention as being conflictual or combative. During this discussion, leaders should follow a three-step approach to the conversation (i.e., a "compliment sandwich"):

1. First, begin with inclusive, supportive, and engaging statements that reinforce how important this group member is to the entire group process

and the leaders: "We wanted to check in with you about how group is going for you. We have enjoyed having you as a part of our group and appreciate your thoughts and feelings. How is the group going for you?"

2. Second, describe specifically what has been observed and invite the disruptive group member to explore and learn from the situation: "We are not sure if you are aware of this or not, but at our last group meeting, we noticed that you seemed tense and frustrated during the group discussion and this may have led you to interrupt group members or cut them off a few times. How are you feeling about the group? What do you think is going on?"

3. Finally, offer positive statements of affirmation and suggestions that may motivate the group member to monitor and change the behavior. These suggestions can include ones that the leaders can take responsibility for as well, "We know you did not intentionally mean to be rude or interruptive; however, we did want to bring it to your attention because it may inadvertently lead others to engage less with you. We see you as a valuable member of our group who actively contributes to group discussions. In the future, would it be helpful for you to sit near me and when you feel the need to share, you can catch my attention? I will be sure to acknowledge that you would like some time and give you the next available opening. Would you be receptive to nonverbal cues from me if you inadvertently interrupt others?"

High-Intensity Intervention Approach

By the time a high-intensity intervention is needed, it is apparent to the student leaders that the group dynamic and cohesiveness are at risk. At this critical point, leaders must fully embrace their positions as respected authorities and leaders of the group. An intervention at this level may be implemented either during the group or again privately with the disruptive member. For example, leaders may need to express an initial warning through immediate feedback during the group discussion by saying, "Excuse me, please try not to interrupt while another group member is speaking." The intervention may escalate to even more direct feedback and requests such as, "Before we continue any further, I think it is best for the group if we take a break for tonight." Ultimately, leaders may need to make an executive decision that the disruptive group member is negatively impacting the group and may no longer be allowed to be a part of the group. Leaders should sit down privately with the group member and explicitly state the situation and resulting outcome. As a follow-up, leaders should be prepared to discuss the situation with the remaining group members and allow adequate time for processing the change, and loss, within the group.

Common Group Issues

Given the complexity and variable dynamic among, and within, groups, predicting how each group will flow and connect may be difficult. The following are common issues that arise within a group context that leaders can anticipate and prepare for (Hunsberger et al., 2003):

Differences in Group Dynamics

Group leaders will find it helpful to anticipate that group dynamics differ significantly across groups. For example, depending on the group members' personalities and communication styles, some groups may connect relatively quickly and develop an active, excitable, enthusiastic style of engagement. Other groups, however, may be more tempered in their dynamic, inviting a more introspective, self-reflective, and quiet atmosphere. Some groups may need more explicit direction and guidance from their student leaders, while other groups may "take the lead" early on in the process and, on occasion, even overpower the student leaders. The "success" of the group is not necessarily indicated by the level of verbal activity during discussions; rather, a more valid indicator for student leaders to attend to when evaluating the productiveness of their group is the degree to which each group member feels supported and connected to the group as a whole. Leaders should be prepared to adjust their leadership style to the needs of the group in a way that promotes group cohesion and connection.

Quiet Group Members

Group leaders may initially perceive quiet group members as being on the periphery of the group. Engaging these group members will require patience and subtle, yet confident, direction from the student leaders. In the beginning, student leaders may find it helpful to rely on a "round-robin" approach, which allows for each group member to be invited to express his or her opinion or response to the student leaders' prompts. Student leaders should be prepared to expect minimal or possibly no response from these quieter group members. In addition, an "I don't know" response may be a more common and "safer" response. Student leaders should not prematurely interpret this type of response as a lack of engagement or connection; rather, the quiet group member may not yet feel comfortable or even know how to articulate a more in-depth response. In addition, the quiet group member may be responding to group dynamics not yet recognized, such as the size of the group or group members that are too talkative or dominating. As the group progresses, student leaders can regularly check in with the quiet group member and offer recurring invitations and encouragement to help habituate the group member to the process. This type of check-in may be conducted one-on-one or within the group itself. For example, the leaders could ask a question such as, "Would it be okay to swing back around and ask more questions later?" to give the group member an opportunity to share with the student leaders where he or she is in the process and also time to consider and prepare for a future interaction. Checking back in with the group member is imperative, especially if the group member is receptive to this request. Alternatively, having student leaders check in with the quiet group member outside of the group may offer a more comfortable environment to share experiences.

Over time, both group members and leaders develop comfort and familiarity that can foster more group participation as the group members who were initially quiet in the early meetings gradually share more over time. In addition, some quiet group members may find the group experience to be rewarding just from listening to the group's dialogue. In those circumstances, leaders can use regular attendance, or even early arrival to group, as a nonverbal indicator of the quiet group member's commitment and connection with the group.

Talkative Group Members

Similar to the initial reaction to quiet group members, leaders may misperceive members who are talkative and who "dominate" the conversation as active contributors who keep up the conversation. However, this early mistake may sacrifice quality of discussion for quantity of comments. Leaders should be attuned to how much of this contribution to the group discussion positively or negatively impacts the other group members. Allowing group members to speak too much runs the potential risk of alienating other group members. Leaders can assess nonverbal responses that signal how the other group members are perceiving this member, including eye rolls, direct verbal disagreements, or withdrawal by folding their arms and avoiding eye contact. Excessive talking by a group member may be related to internal, underlying issues, such as social anxiety or a high need to self-disclose due to emotional distress. Leaders can balance the excessiveness by interjecting in a way that does not abruptly silence the talkative member, but encourages other group members to step in. For example, leaders may interject, "I'm sorry to interrupt, but I feel what you are saying is important and I want to check in with the rest of the group about their thoughts and feelings to what you are saying." Alternatively, if leaders can tell the talkative member is nominating multiple points of interest but not allowing time to process them all, leaders may gently interrupt and say, "Let me step in quickly for a brief moment because I believe you are hitting on a number of important areas others may relate to. Let me put a pin where you are and check in with others about what you have said so far, and then we can continue." Of course, a more direct approach may be needed if subtle redirection is not successful. Leaders should not be afraid to offer this feedback to protect the cohesion and integrity of the group. In fact, this talkative member may likely have received similar feedback in the past and could continue to benefit from feedback and instruction from trusted and respected peers.

Emotional Distress

Group leaders should expect that tension and emotional distress may be experienced by some members of the group. This type of emotive response is not a barrier or negative contributor to the dynamic of the group; rather, it can present an opportunity to raise the quality of the conversation and depth of the emotional experience of the group if modulated appropriately. Sensitive topics, individual frustrations (e.g., "stressed out" or "venting"), or misinterpretations within the group are possible triggers for eliciting normative emotional distress in some individual members. When these types of conversations take place within the group, they demonstrate the group's progressive development toward cohesion. Leaders must acknowledge that they are not professionally trained clinicians; however, in relatively benign and normative situations of stress, leaders and group members can offer valuable support to the distressed group member through displays of sympathy and empathy. In addition, both leaders and group members may offer suggestions for strategies that may assist the distressed group member. For example, one strategy leaders can offer is a referral to a professional trained in dealing with significant and serious situations (e.g., psychologist, university administrator, etc.).

Side Conversations

Research has indicated both positive and negative outcomes related to dyadic side conversations in small groups (Swaab, Phillips, Diermeier, & Husted Medvec, 2008). In some cases, side conversations facilitate the formation of factions within the group; in others, the absence of side conversations enhances the unity of the group. The benefits of side conversations may depend upon the tasks and ultimate goals of the group (Swaab et al., 2008). Early on, leaders can expect some side conversations as certain group members may know each other better than others. In some respects, side conversations may offer early on an immediate sense of connection and inclusion in this new group experience. However, leaders need to be mindful that over time, other group members may begin to feel excluded as factions begin to develop within the group. Leaders may need to use low-level interventions to bring the dyad back to the group discussion, such as subtly reminding them of the group guidelines about respect and interruption.

Violation of the Group's "Ground Rules"

One guideline that unfortunately is commonly violated is maintaining confidentiality, or privacy, of the group's discussions. Another guideline may be using electronic devices during the group meeting. The immediate availability of information due to the sophisticated technology of smartphones and tablets produces important communication and dynamic challenges for leaders facilitating meaningful group discussions. Every effort should be made to minimize and avoid these types of violations. For example, leaders can take the lead from the beginning and review the "ground rules," or guidelines for the group, in the first session. If a violation occurs, leaders must evaluate the severity of the violation and its impact on the group. In minor infractions, leaders may do a general review with all group members to refresh them of the core guidelines that all participants abide by and the rationale behind them. Should a more serious infraction occur, such as the clear violation of confidentiality or direct disrespect of another group member, the leaders should speak directly with the offending group member privately. The group may possibly suggest violations for discussion with the entire group. In this case, the group may benefit from the positive challenge of having a healthy discourse about the conflict and seek resolution of the issue together.

Conflict between Group Members

Leaders can expect normative disruption and tension between group members as comfort and cohesion deepen within the group. As more information becomes available and idiosyncrasies begin to emerge, differences and disagreements add depth and complexity to the group dynamic. As tensions build, leaders need to assess the situation and evaluate the "pulse" of the group by observing group members' reactions and comments as the discussion continues. On one hand, allowing the discussion to continue serves as an opportunity to experience how the group "rallies" or works through the situation together. However, delaying an intervention and stepping in too late runs the risk of leaving the group fractured and disconnected. In the "heat of the moment," leaders are advised to intervene in a manner that is most appropriate for reducing the tension as effectively and efficiently as possible. For example, leaders may interrupt and insert themselves into the dialogue by stating the following, "It appears to me that topic has activated quite a few feelings and thoughts. It shows me how passionate and important this topic is for many of us here. Why don't we take a few minutes to take a step back and hear how others are experiencing the group right now?" Leaders need to evaluate which intervention approach is best to protect the dynamic and cohesion of the group.

Relationships Outside of the Group

Group members and leaders may indicate interest in associating outside of the group setting. These relationships are normative and even expected to occur as intimacy and familiarity within the group setting develop. Leaders should address this normative issue from the beginning when reviewing the guidelines and rationale of the group. At times, leaders may need to contact their group members outside of group. For example, leaders are encouraged to reach out to absent group members to check on them and share how they were missed and are valued when they attend group. In addition, leaders may have to meet with individual group members to discuss a group-related issue (e.g., disruption within the group) that may not be appropriate to discuss in the presence of the entire group. Moreover, a group member may contact one or both leaders to discuss their experience of the group and considerations for future commitment and attendance. Only issues not appropriate to discuss within the group merit outside contact between leaders and group members. Finally, it is appropriate for leaders and group members to connect for a culminating experience that indicates the group is truly adjourning. For example, leaders and group members may wish to have a celebratory dinner together outside of their usual group meeting place.

CHAPTER 7

Transition to University

An Applied Group Experience

For groups to be effective, all members must commit themselves to cooperation and achievement. The success of a group and its outcomes are dependent upon three basic, yet essential, factors: clarity of the group's purpose and goals, positive and motivated cooperation among group members, and most importantly trust. The T2U program serves as an applied example of how to incorporate these principles into a successful group dynamic experience.

The Transition to University Program

The transition to university life is a significant event for incoming first-year students. One would be hard-pressed to identify a more challenging and pivotal life change in young adulthood so impactful on multiple areas of emerging adult development. These areas of development include academics, social, activities of daily living, and overall quality of life. First, students experience a significant shift in academic challenges that include more difficult course material, higher expectations of academic performance, new and unique assessment measures, larger classes, and less interaction and support from instructors (e.g., lecture-style instruction). Second, first-year university students experience a radically different social landscape surrounded by peers who, for the most part, are new and have no familiarity or prior affiliation other than attending the same college campus. The social demands inherent in this new setting are coupled with the challenge of effectively implementing social skills to evolve superficial social interactions into deep and meaningful relationships. Finally, the demands of navigating and maintaining activities of daily living as an independent young adult significantly increase.

For many first-year students, their primary and early experiences of living away from home may have been attending summer camp for a few short weeks or periodic sleepovers with peers. Instead, first-year university students can now expect to cope with a variety of daily living tasks, such as conflict with roommates, managing their personal finances, doing laundry, and developing and maintaining a healthy, balanced schedule of self-regulation (i.e., meals, exercise, and sleep). Embedded throughout this experience are the additional challenges of making decisions regarding one's future career, developing and maintaining a long-term romantic relationship, and coping with notable changes in the parent–child dynamic as the young adult begins to experience more autonomy and individuation (Mattanah, Hancock & Brand, 2004).

All of these factors occurring simultaneously in a concentrated amount of time will have an impact on young adults. For example, first-year college students may undergo the psychological experience of homesickness as they are suddenly displaced and disconnected from the familiarity of previous social supports and surroundings. The experience of such an acute separation has been associated with academic and social consequences (Scopelliti & Tiberio, 2010; Sun, Hagedorn, & Zhang, 2016; Thurber & Walton, 2012). In addition, these emerging young adults report experiences of depression (Wolf, Scurria, & Webster, 1998), increased substance use (White et al., 2005; White, Labouvie, & Papadaratsakis, 2005), and loneliness (Cutrona, 1982). In fact, 75 percent of incoming first-year students reported loneliness at least some of the time (Cutrona, 1982).

One of the most effective ways of addressing these normative transition issues is to facilitate an incoming student's sense of belonging and perception that the university "fits" or matches the student (Watt & Badger, 2009; Wintre et al., 2008). For example, universities can provide incoming students with opportunities to engage in social activities and campus resources as quickly as possible. Another method of addressing these issues is the use of peer support groups. Mattanah et al. (2010) found higher levels of social support for both genders and lower levels of loneliness the semester following participation in the support group when compared to a control group. In addition, students who participated in a support group had higher GPAs in the first semester of their sophomore year compared to the control group.

Connecting with a peer group within the first year of university life can have a positive long-term impact beyond just the first year. Pancer and his colleagues (2004) reported compelling evidence from their longitudinal examination of fourth-year, senior-level students who had been randomly assigned at the beginning of their first year at university to either a peer support group or a control condition. This peer support group, comprised of two upper-class student leaders and approximately 8-10 first-year students, met regularly throughout their first semester at university for a total of nine meetings. In their fourth year of study, students from the control and intervention groups completed several measures of adjustment related to university life. The results indicated significant long-term effects for the intervention with those who had participated in the support groups showing significantly better adjustment to university than those in the control group in their fourth year of study. Moreover, results indicated successful retention of students by their fourth year. Only 7.8 percent of students who had participated in the peer support groups during their first year left the university without completing a degree compared to 28 percent of those in the control group who left the university without completing a degree.

With the support of Dr. Pancer and his colleagues, the T2U program was implemented at Queens University of Charlotte in the fall of 2006. The 2006 T2U pilot program began with 18 first-year students placed into three peer support groups. These groups were coled by six upper-class students. Group facilitators participated in a three-hour training session that focused on the facilitating group dynamics and preparing for the first group meeting. Each week for the nine weeks of the program, the student leaders and the program directors received guidance and directed supervision from Dr. Pancer who provided a training guide that was adapted for the program at Queens (Hunsberger et al., 2003). Since its inception in 2006, the T2U program has grown rapidly at Queens to approximately 140 first-year students participating in 16 T2U groups each fall. These groups continue to be coled by a leadership team of approximately 32 upper-class students enrolled in a leadership and group dynamic course. First-year students in this program who were more strongly connected and positive about their peer group were less lonely, felt more social support, and indicated greater adjustment to university life compared to those who were less connected with their peer support group (Harper & Allegretti, 2009b). Moreover, first-year students who participated in this program had higher retention rates compared to first-year students who did not participate (Harper & Allegretti, 2009a; 2013).

The Purpose and Goals of the T2U Group

The purpose of each T2U group is to provide an opportunity for first-year students to discuss different topics related to their new life. The group context provides a safe and confidential setting that promotes social support and connection among its student group members. These discussions are facilitated by upper-class student leaders on campus to enhance the first-year students' connection with the rest of the university community. The topics for discussion focus on academic, social, and personal factors of overall adjustment. The goals of each group meeting, and the overall program, are to increase social connection, offer support and information, and improve student adjustment in multiple areas related to university life.

At the first meeting, the rationale and guidelines of the program are shared with the first-year group members. The student coleaders frequently reference these important aspects of the program throughout the group experience to remind and reinforce the purpose and goals of the group. Guidelines for the group include how to interact respectfully with each group member, how to solve logistical issues such as cell phone use and attendance, and how to protect and maintain confidentiality.

Design and Size of Group

The T2U program is specifically designed for incoming first-year students. Although it is possible to implement the program on a short-term basis during the first semester of the first-year student's academic year, the program and group meetings may be expanded and continued to the second spring semester (Harper & Allegretti, 2009; 2013). While the program has a targeted focus on specific content areas of adjustment, such as forming new social ties and adopting healthy life habits, flexibility in the program allows response to group members' needs as they evolve.

A recommended group size is between five and ten group members, with the ideal number being seven group members (Yalom, 1975; Yalom & Leszcz, 2005). This number of group members allows for sufficient quality and quantity of communication and interaction while anticipating factors that may impact the group's dynamic, such as possible absences or interconflict among group members. In addition, the group is led by two upper-class students who have received preliminary training in group dynamics and leadership skills focused on facilitating quality discussion and group cohesion. The upper-class student leaders continue to receive ongoing supervision and instruction from a faculty member trained in group dynamics and facilitation throughout the T2U practicum experience (Harper & Allegretti, 2015).

Session Outline of Program

The session topics and outline of the program are intentionally designed with first-year students and their university life in mind. When considering the numerous challenges the first-year student faces, it is imperative that the session topics themselves are personally relevant and normative to each group member. In addition, the timing of these session topics is key for encouraging group cohesion, communication, and ongoing peer support to mitigate these challenges. Common issues and concerns for the first-year student are homesickness and social belonging, academic concerns and grade performance, roommate conflict, financial concerns, and anxiety over choosing a major. When considering these common challenges and the timeline in which they emerge, aligning the session topics within this timeline is essential for engaging and supporting the first-year student. An example of a session outline below illustrates this point:

Week # in Fall Semester

1	Session 1:	Introduction and Expectations about University Life
2	Session 2:	New Friends and Who's Who on Campus?
3	Session 3:	Balancing Act: Academics and Social Lives

Environment of Group Setting

The atmosphere and environment of the group setting play a subtle role in facilitating group cohesion and communication. Ideally, the setting in which the group discussion takes place is one that is soothing, inviting, and conducive to personal and intimate discussions. For example, using low or dimmed lighting and soft couches and chairs within a circle serve to promote inclusion, connection, and distinct separation from the outside world. Additional elements such as food and drinks at each meeting enhance the interactive quality of the experience.

Seating Arrangements of the Group

Much has been written about how the seating arrangement of the group can impact the quality of the interaction and connection among group members (Brotherton, 2010; Hendrick, Geisen, & Coy, 1974; Sommer, 1967; Burgoon, 2003). Some studies have indicated that group members who sit side by side are less likely to talk than group members who are face-to-face or more centrally located to maximize eye contact (Michelini, Passalacqua, & Cusimano, 1976; Silverstein & Stang, 1976; Steinzor, 1950). Moreover, the seating arrangement can affect the leaders' perception of group members' nonverbal communication cues such as body posture, lean, and orientation. In addition, the study of proxemics and its related concepts of interpersonal space and territoriality suggest that the quality of group members' interactions can be impacted by group members' perceptions of ownership of the space and personal space (Hall,

1982). For example, personal space can influence likability and related-ness with those in positions of authority (Kelly, 1972).

Where the leaders sit can influence how group members perceive them as leaders and as part of the group. Howells and Becker (1962) indicated those with the ability to maximize direct eye contact may exert greater control and more active participation in the verbal exchange compared to those with more limited ability to make direct eye contact. Leaders must be able to make clear and unobstructed eye contact with each other, but also with group members. A circular seating arrangement is ideal to promote more interaction and accessibility to each group member and the leaders.

Recruitment of Group Members

As stated earlier, the purpose of the T2U program is to assist incoming first-year students with the transition and adjustment to university life. As such, groups are primarily comprised of traditional first-year students; however, international and transfer students may benefit from this experience as well. When making decisions about group composition, an important consideration is to determine the primary purpose and goals of the group and how each student would benefit from participation and inclusion. With this in mind, the initial task at hand is to contact and recruit group members.

One of the most effective methods of connecting with the entire class of incoming first-year students is to send a letter to their e-mail address prior to their arrival on campus. The first-year student receives information about the program in the e-mail and is invited to sign up for the experience online. While this method is financially economical and time-efficient, some recipients may not view the message due to spam blocks or infrequent checks of their e-mail. Another method for recruit-ment through electronic means is to post information fliers about the program on online forums, such as the school's Facebook page, website, or other electronic-based bulletin boards designed for student announce-ments or other information. In addition, the T2U facilitators who also serve simultaneously as resident assistants (RAs) or orientation leaders

(OLs) may encourage recruitment by posting information on their personal online page or through other social media outlets.

A more traditional method of contact and recruitment is to post fliers either on campus or included in orientation and acceptance packets. Prioritizing areas of high volume for placement on campus is strategically imperative, since many students may disregard or miss the posting among multiple advertisements filling a board. Suggested areas are residence halls that are typically filled with incoming first-year students, campus advising offices, counseling centers or other offices of academic support, and student recreational areas.

Another method of recruitment relies on the immediate and established sources of information on campus. These sources include faculty, student life support staff, university administrators, and previous participants and facilitators of the T2U program. For example, upper-class students who serve as RAs or OLs share and recommend this program to incoming first-year students as part of their hall or orientation programs. Using these peer advocates as representatives of the program may increase both the credibility and merit of the program and motivate more first-year students to participate. University administrators and faculty who are informed and support the program may invite representatives of the program to present briefly at the start of their classes. Some faculty may even offer extra credit to enhance motivation to participate.

Organized opportunities, such as a designated hour during orientation week, to present information directly to first-year students about the program are also influential in securing participants. This method also allows interested first-year students to ask questions and meet current T2U student leaders. One successful recruitment strategy has been to display an information table immediately outside the dining hall or other student community areas during scheduled meal and event times. Representatives of the program, such as current T2U leaders, sit at the table in paired shifts during high-traffic hours, such as meal times. Sign-up sheets with designated meeting times are available for interested first-year students to complete right away with their contact information. First-year students often spontaneously sign up individually or even in groups with whom they are eating. This recruitment method is even more likely to be successful when first-year students are encouraged by engaging and enthusiastic T2U leaders sitting right by the dining hall entrance door.

At the time of recruitment, interested potential group members select an evening meeting time that fits best with their schedule. These group meeting times are designated by upper-class student leaders and are pre-arranged by the program coordinator prior to the start of recruitment. Group meetings are held throughout the week from Monday through Thursday evenings, and the expected meeting time for each meeting is at least 60–90 minutes. For example, Monday evening groups may be held from 6:00 to 7:30 pm or 7:30 to 9:00 pm. Depending on availability of space, multiple group meetings can be held simultaneously.

Leaders in the program are provided with a roster of interested group members to contact in preparation for the first group meeting. Contact methods include phone, e-mail, text, and social media. All participants are confirmed for their requested meeting time if space is available. In addition, participants are provided their peer leaders' names, contact information, and details of the first meeting (i.e., date and time, location, etc.).

Once the first meeting has commenced, student leaders will maintain engagement and management of their group members throughout the program and semesters. Social media outlets such as Facebook and texting are the most popular methods of connection. Each week, student leaders reach out with reminders and details for the next group meeting. In addition, leaders may voluntarily touch base with their group members about how their week is going or even share a meal together outside of the organized group session. Regular contact and engagement serve to maintain motivation and connection with the group experience. In addition, ongoing contact promotes social inclusion and a sense of community throughout the year.

Format of Group Discussion Meetings

A typical format for group discussion meetings has four main parts: a check-in, a general discussion on the session topic of the week, an activity focused on the session topic, and finally a wrap-up and evaluation of the session meeting (see Hunsberger et al., 2003). These four parts are designed for the group to meet identified goals for each meeting. In addition, the format of each session encourages group cohesion and more detailed and personal disclosure. Of course, as the group dynamic evolves through stages of connection and cohesion, leaders may begin to rely less on the organized activities included in each session and instead allow additional time and space for more personal disclosure during check-in and general discussion.

Check-In

The purpose of the check-in is to provide a time for group members and leaders to share their personal thoughts and feelings openly. Members are encouraged to be self-reflective and share their experiences since the last meeting. The check-in may also be an opportunity to follow up on previous issues or provide updates on identified goals. Leaders may "model" how to check-in with group members by sharing about their own week and inviting questions and feedback from group members. A number of tactics may be used to encourage participation and elicit information from each group member. Examples of methods include the following:

1. *Round-robin.* This method refers to beginning with one group member and going in a circular manner or sequential pattern around the group.
2. *Popcorn.* This technique can be modified in a number of ways to promote check-in. One way to use this technique is to invite members to just "pop up" and speak when the opening presents itself. Another alternative is to invite a group member who has recently completed their check-in to spontaneously call upon or "pop" a fellow group member and invite them to begin check-in.
3. *Echo.* This method encourages group members to listen for personal details that mimic or "echo" their own self-reflection. Once the group members identify a common experience, they are encouraged to follow that group member's check-in by "echoing" similar thoughts and feelings. For example, a group member may share what a difficult week he or she had due to a recent midterm examination. Another group member who took the same examination "echoes" a similar or related thought and feeling to that class experience.

Over time and as the group becomes more cohesive, the time for check-in tends to expand as group members become more comfortable initiating discussion on their own. To facilitate this cohesion and increased comfort, the leaders may rely on the following list of questions commonly used each week as group members begin to learn the process of the group:

1. How has your week been?
2. What stands out to you about your week that you would like to us to know?
3. Is there anything you would like advice or support on?
4. Which experiences were the best and worst of the week: the "Highs and Lows of the week" or "Rose and Thorn of the week?"
5. Are there any comments about the session last week?
6. Does anyone have any progress or updates on personal goals?

General Discussion

The general discussion provides a time for group members and leaders to delve more deeply into the session topic as it relates to their personal experience. Group members are encouraged to be self-reflective and share either their current or previous experience as it relates to the session topic. Since the session topics are time-sensitive, they are scheduled in a manner coordinated with campus life. For example, one of the session topics held in the early weeks of the fall semester focuses on making new friends and connecting with resources on campus. For the general discussion, first-year student group members are invited to talk about their early social connections and receive information from their student leaders about academic and social resources on campus. In addition, the leaders may again "model" by sharing their own personal experiences related to the topic and invite group members to ask questions or offer feedback. For example, leaders may recommend campus activities or organizations to join that they found personally rewarding for the social experiences.

Activity for Session Topic

Following the general discussion of the session topic, student leaders shift to a more instructional role in the group process. Leaders share brief educational information on the topic in a didactic manner to their group members. Leaders then present the activity or exercise related to the topic. The activity provides group members with a structured goal and shared task while also offering helpful strategies and suggestions to improve group members' experience related to the topic. In addition, the activity promotes group cohesion and social connection by inviting all group members to participate in this structured activity.

As an illustration, in the group activity for the T2U session topic focused on "New Friends and Who's Who on Campus," leaders educate their first-year student group members about a variety of opportunities that may result in increased social connections. These opportunities are both on campus and in the community. In addition, group members are invited to share with each other and their leaders their top five new acquaintances and how they established those early social connections. Leaders offer specific strategies for follow-up and maintenance of these newly formed friendships.

Wrap-up and Evaluation

At the end of each session meeting, student leaders summarize the discussion by identifying the key points. Ideally, the leaders also share general observations of commonalities across group members and emphasize positive statements or actions of group members during the meeting. Leaders also invite feedback and questions from group members to wrap up the discussion. Before transitioning to the evaluation portion of the meeting, leaders share the topic of the next week's discussion and encourage group members to give some thought over the next week in preparation for next week's session. Finally, leaders distribute the evaluation forms to the group members to complete before leaving. Group members do not put any personal identification on these forms, and they are encouraged to express their thoughts and feelings about the meeting in a confidential manner. Leaders also complete evaluation forms for the session. The completed forms are collected as group members leave the room.

CHAPTER 8

Practicum in Group Dynamics

A Supervision Course

Supervision is an essential component for student leaders to learn how to implement their leadership skills effectively and confidently. Participation in supervision sessions offers multiple benefits to the novice leader. One benefit of supervision between the supervisor and the student leaders is for the supervisor to learn of potential issues among leaders or group members before these issues are exacerbated. At that time, the supervisor can offer informed advice and suggestions on how best to handle these issues. Supervision is especially helpful when conducted in a group or classroom setting. This group supervision can normalize student leaders' experiences as they gain confidence and knowledge of how to effectively facilitate group discussions while providing a forum and opportunity to demonstrate support for each other during this learning process.

A structured experiential course on leadership and group dynamics is especially useful and effective at utilizing supervision as part of the teaching paradigm (Harper & Allegretti, 2015). This approach to learning group dynamics and leadership skills relies on an interdisciplinary approach to learning and implementing concepts through real-world application. The objective of this course is to teach advanced undergraduate students leadership skills and group dynamics through specific, organized classroom activities and participatory types of applied group experiences. Supervision and applied group experiences allow for a more complete integration of learning and support as student leaders begin to apply their new skills.

The following are three primary areas where supervision of leaders can be effectively incorporated into the practicum course:

1. Students leaders may participate as group members in a process-oriented group experience led by an instructor trained in group dynamics and facilitation.
2. Students leaders may participate as students in a didactic, discussion-based classroom seminar about topics related to coleadership and group dynamics.
3. Students leaders may colead their own discussion group comprised of student peers.

Student Leaders as Group Members

One of the most effective ways for students to learn how to lead a group discussion is for them to participate as group members themselves. This training model is most commonly used in clinical-based courses, such as a graduate-level course on group psychotherapy (Eichler, 1987; Halgin, 1982). In the practicum course, student leaders participate in a weekly process-oriented group experience facilitated by a trained supervisor, instructor, or faculty member. In other words, the students in the class serve as members of their own group where the instructor can intentionally demonstrate and integrate knowledge of leadership and communication skills, and supervision of group dynamics and concepts. Participating in an experiential group as a group member offers novice student leaders "in vivo" exposure to the group dynamic process and techniques (Hulse-Killacky, 1996; Riva & Korinek, 2004). For example, the instructor can organize and conduct the process group in the same four-part sequence the student leaders will implement when they lead their own groups: check-in, group discussion, relevant exercise or activities, and wrap-up. This sequence will be a familiar outline and preparatory review to student leaders when facilitating their own peer groups.

During check-in, student leaders share a concise narrative summarizing aspects of their personal experiences from the previous week to the group. Ideally, student leaders share relevant content related to their personal or professional goals. For example, senior-class student leaders may elect to share their progress on completing applications for employment or graduate school upon graduation. The instructor or supervisor demonstrates facilitation techniques that encourage the group's connection and quality of discussion about these personal reflections.

Following check-in, group members are encouraged to use group time by suggesting an issue for discussion. This issue may be personal and specific in nature or it may be an overall theme or topic to which all group members can likely relate. For example, group members who are juniors may elect to discuss how they are balancing their work and social lives now that there is a notable increase in both work and academic demands since their sophomore year at the university. The instructor facilitates the discussion to highlight common themes and connection among group members. Group members are encouraged to brainstorm solutions or strategies with their peers as part of an interactive exercise. The instructor's leadership skills and style offer opportunities to illustrate concepts of group dynamics (e.g., storming, norming, group identity). For example, the instructor may model for students how to negotiate conflict among group members and how to use nonverbal cues as a way to demonstrate engagement with the group. As illustration, consider the following scenario:

> One of the student leaders shares with the group and instructor a struggle with procrastination on completing academic class assignments because of prioritizing job applications and searching for job opportunities. The instructor notices a number of other student leaders in the group nodding in empathy and agreement. The instructor states to the group, "I notice many of you appear to relate to what is being shared. Would any of you like to share what you are thinking or feeling about this?" After further discussion, the instructor directs the group toward problem-solving and solutions by stating, "Given so many of you have experienced what is being described, is there anyone here who would like to share a successful strategy for dealing with this type of issue?"

In this scenario, the instructor demonstrates how to use nonverbal behaviors as cues to invite connection and participation within the group. At the end of the session, the instructor may summarize the overall group experience and invite students to identify and evaluate the group's discussion for themes and concepts related to group dynamics. This supervisory, "in vivo" modeling experience allows for the opportunity to review leadership strategies and resolve issues that occurred during their group discussions. For example, the instructor may ask student leaders to consider how they might have coled the discussion differently. Student leaders can imagine how similar interactions or issues may arise in their own groups and brainstorm and prepare for how they might handle those issues. Finally, assigning weekly process notes of the group meetings may enhance the learning and critical thinking skills of the group process. Specifically, student leaders can review and evaluate a number of elements of the group experience, including their role in the group, the composition and tasks of the group, the development and evolution of the group over time, and the strengths and weaknesses of the group.

Student Leaders as Students

For the didactic supervision experience, student leaders participate in a discussion-based classroom seminar weekly. This class follows the more traditional instructional style commonly found in advanced undergraduate- or graduate-level seminars. Each week, students are asked to read empirically based journal articles or other relevant readings on topics related to leadership and group dynamics. For example, student leaders early in the process may find articles on the development of coleader relationship and the characteristics of dyadic interaction useful (Atieno Okech & Kline, 2006; Fall & Wejnert, 2005; Miles & Kivlighan, 2010; Nosko & Wallace, 1997). The supervisor instructs the students on key concepts, themes, and how to utilize this information when coleading their own peer group discussion.

In addition to these concept-based readings, student leaders are also asked to read articles specific to their group members' experiences. For example, student leaders coleading a peer group of first-year college students may find articles on the first-year college transition helpful to incorporate into their group discussion (e.g., Buote et al., 2007; Davidson, Feldman, & Margalit, 2012; Johnson, Gans, Kerr, & LaValle, 2010; Mattanah et al., 2010, 2012). Ideally, the supervisor or instructor should arrange the empirical articles in such a way that the student leaders are able to review and discuss the material prior to the student-led group meetings. For example, an article on violence victimization on campus and the culture of college "hook-ups" may be read and discussed in the advanced seminar class prior to the student-led discussion on romantic relationships within their own peer groups (e.g., Tomsich, Schaible, Rennison, & Gover, 2013). Key strategies and information identified and discussed in the seminar class may then be useful for sharing in an appropriate manner in the student-led group meetings.

Finally, the most integral part of the supervision process is the actual supervision of the student-led groups by the trained instructor. Each pair of student coleaders is required to maintain written process notes of each group meeting and provide an oral presentation weekly about their group meeting to their fellow coleaders and the trained instructor. Typically, student coleaders may begin with an oral summary of the group's discussion and then expand upon specific group members or dynamics about the group. Their weekly process notes not only provide content, but also address the process of the group. These process notes may include specific members' behaviors, group dynamics, patterns, and themes emerging within the group. An outline of questions assists the student leaders with their writing and critical thinking skills of the group process. For example, student leaders are asked to consider the sequence of events that occurred during the group meeting and the quality of the communication and participation of group members. In addition, student leaders are asked to describe their own thoughts and feelings about the group and the role they placed as leaders. At the end of the semester, student leaders are required to write a final evaluative analysis of their observations of the group process that is a summary of their overall conclusions about the group dynamics.

Students as Leaders

The practicum is the applied group experience where student leaders now have an opportunity to practice their leadership skills in their own peer support groups. These student-led groups are conducted separate and apart from the seminar and "in vivo group" experiences. Note that the trained instructor is not present during these meetings and the student coleaders are solely responsible for the development and facilitation of their groups.

As illustration, the T2U program (Harper & Allegretti, 2009, 2013; Pancer, Pratt, Hunsberger, & Alisat, 2004; Pancer, Pratt, & Alisat, 2006) serves as the applied component for the Practicum in Group Dynamics course conducted at Queens University of Charlotte. As described previously, student leaders are placed in pairs and required to colead groups of approximately 10 first-year students. Groups are scheduled to meet weekly for the first 10 weeks of the first semester of college. These groups resume meeting in the spring semester following the winter break. The spring sessions take place weekly for the first 10 weeks of the second semester of the first year of college. These group meetings are held in the evening with refreshments to promote attendance and in a relaxed and private setting created specifically for this program. Student leaders collect a variety of data and information to bring with them to their supervision session following the evening meeting. For example, student leaders collect data on group members' attendance and evaluations about the group meeting. In addition, student leaders write process notes outlining the group discussion and dynamics of the meeting.. The student leaders write about the sequence of events during the meeting, the communication and level of participation for each group member, the roles of group members (e.g., who is emerging as a leader), and the dynamic of the group (e.g., "stuck" versus a productive direction). Student leaders then offer an oral and written presentation on their group during the supervision session conducted in their advanced seminar class.

Case Example: A Three-Day Supervision on Procrastination

Procrastination, or the delay initiating or completing effortful tasks that often result in discomfort and anxiety, is a common experience among university students. Balancing both academic and social lives as an independent, emerging young adult is a normative challenge for most university students, and this challenge often manifests itself throughout students' higher-education experience (Solomon & Rothblum, 1984;

Onwuegbuzie, 2004). The problem may not be as simple as difficulty with time management or other executive functioning abilities; rather, procrastination is a complex psychological experience of affective, behavioral, and cognitive factors often associated with serious, and negative, consequences (Fee & Tangney, 2000; Tice & Baumeister, 1997). In the T2U program at Queens University of Charlotte, student leaders facilitate a discussion about procrastination among their first-year peer support group members. In preparation for leading this discussion, student leaders participate in a three-day supervision class experience on the topic of procrastination.

Day 1: Class Instruction on the Topic and Strategies

In preparation for the upcoming peer group discussion on procrastination, student leaders are required to read articles on procrastination and to participate in a didactic seminar discussion of those articles. During the discussion, student leaders learn about the association between hope and academic procrastination and how hope coupled with a clear plan is optimal at reducing procrastination when a specific goal is identified (Alexander & Onwuegbuzie, 2007). Moreover, student leaders discuss the role of goal focus and the type of focus (e.g., process vs outcome) as they relate to procrastination and goal pursuits (Krause & Freund, 2014). In addition, students learn to identify which type of procrastinator a student may be, such as an active versus passive procrastinator, and identify specific strategies of time management and sequential organization of assignments (Chun Chu & Choi, 2005). With this information, student leaders can then suggest concepts and strategies to their first-year students to help cope with the normative challenge of procrastination.

Day 2: Student Leaders' Process Group

As described previously, student leaders participate as group members in their own process group. This group is led by the faculty member or instructor trained in group facilitation and group dynamics. On Day 2 of supervision training, the faculty leader facilitates a group discussion on procrastination among the junior- and senior-level student leaders. This process group begins with a "check-in" which allows student leaders to talk about their previous week and personal experiences. The discussion during this group session focuses on identifying issues that student leaders are avoiding (e.g., "What are you avoiding?"). For some student leaders, these may include relationship conflicts, class assignments and/or grades, or finances. For others, it may be the normative time-sensitive topics of delaying applications to graduate school or developing plans following graduation from the university. During the discussion, the faculty instructor can assist student leaders with identifying situations or examples that illustrate concepts from the required readings. For example, student leaders may identify an academic task on which they are procrastinating, and the faculty instructor can facilitate the discussion to explore more in-depth whether or not the example of procrastination illustrates the associated factors of hope or type of goal focus. In a group activity, student leaders may explore ways that they can motivate themselves to deal with the issue. This activity may include a review of time management skills or brainstorming and sharing strategies for coping with procrastination. The session ends with an overview of the session and the group process. Student leaders are expected to think critically about the group experience and how they might lead their own peer support groups in a similar manner.

Day 3: Supervision of Student-Led Peer Support Group

During the week, student leaders will have coled their peer support group comprised of first-year students as part of their applied practicum course experience. On Day 3 of the supervisory class, student leaders present to the instructor and their class a description of their peer support group discussion. The expectation is that student leaders will have directed their peer support group to explore procrastination and discussed factors and strategies that may be helpful in reducing procrastination. By hearing each group's report and feedback, fellow student leaders may learn new ideas and strategies about how to improve the facilitation and leadership of this topic within their own groups.

The Practicum in Group Dynamics course provides ongoing supervision for the student leaders in three ways. First, student leaders learn through modelling their instructor's behaviors in a process-oriented group experience. Second, student leaders study group dynamics in a traditional class setting. And, third, student leaders learn how to lead groups *in vivo* by leading their own group each week. The structure provides students with the necessary support for them to deal with the complexities of the group experience.

CHAPTER 9

Conclusion

Developing and using students as peer leaders can be influential at the higher-education level. Student leaders can be successful role models who are companions for the entering students on their odyssey through their first year of university. They are able to engage their mentees through shared experiences in a way that experts and professionals are not able to do. Because of these shared experiences, the student leaders are able to delve into topics that are serious and complex while, in many cases, also normative in college transition. These shared experiences can provide the social support that integrates the incoming students into the university and involves them in meaningful deliberation concerning social and emotional issues of emerging adulthood as well as negotiating the challenges of this new academic world.

Students need a clearly defined methodology and training to be effective leaders in higher education. Training includes the essentials of group dynamics, leadership techniques, and prescribed ways of fostering a safe and cohesive social environment. In addition, becoming a leader goes beyond the instruction found within a traditional classroom setting. Student leaders need an applied practicum experience that allows them to develop and implement these leadership techniques and receive ongoing supervision and training to enhance their skillset and confidence.

This book highlights opportunities for strategic interventions and programs that maximize young adult development. For instance, students may develop into campus leaders who promote social inclusion and a sense of belonging, and who assist incoming first-year students with the transition to their new life on campus. One specific program referenced is the T2U program. This program offers student leaders the opportunity to educate and support incoming first-year students within a group context throughout their first academic year at the university level. The program emphasizes the normative issues related to first-year students' transition to their new life on campus. In Book 2 of this series, the manual for the fall and spring semester program will be presented with specific topics, leadership techniques, and strategies to support incoming students during their first year on campus. The manual provides clear guidelines and recommendations for how to implement this type of program at higher-level institutions.

References

Alexander, E. S. and Onwuegbuzie, A. J. (2007). Academic procrastination and the role of hope as a coping strategy. *Personality and Individual Differences, 42,* 1301–1310. https://doi.org/10.1016/j.paid.2006.10.008

Allan, S. S., Bland, C. J., and Dawson, S. J. (1990). A mini-workshop to train medical students to use a patient-centered approach to smoking cessation. *American Journal of Preventative Medicine, 6,* 28–33. Retrieved from PubMed.gov.

Asgari, S. and Frederick, C. (2016). Peer mentors can improve academic performance: A quasi-experimental study of peer mentorship in introductory courses. *Teaching of Psychology, 43,* 131–136. https://doi .org/10.1177/0098628316636288

Astin, A. W. (1977). *Four critical years: Effects of college on beliefs, attitudes, and knowledge.* San Francisco: Jossey-Bass Publishers.

Atieno Okech, J. E. and Kline, W. B. (2006). Competency concerns in group co-leader relationships. *Journal for Specialists in Group Work, 3,* 165–180. https://doi.org/10.1080/01933920500493829

Barchas, P. (1986). A sociophysiological orientation to small groups. In E. Lawler (Ed.), *Advances in group processes* (pp. 209–246). Greenwich, CT: JAI Press.

Baumeister, R. F. and Leary, M. R. (1995). The need to belong: Desire for interpersonal attachments as a fundamental human motivation. *Psychological Bulletin, 117,* 497–529. https://doi.org/10.1037 /0033-2909.117.3.497

Beatrice, J. and Shively, P. (2007). Peer mentors target unique populations; increase use of campus resources. *eSource for College Transitions, 4(5),* 1, 3, 5. Retrieved from http://sc.edu/fye/esource/archive.html

Becker, C., Bull, S., Schaumberg, K., Cauble, A., and Franco, A. (2008). Effectiveness of peer-led eating disorders prevention: A replication trial. *Journal of Consulting and Clinical Psychology, 76,* 347–354. https://doi.org/10.1037/0022-006X.76.2.347

Becker, C., Smith, L. and Ciao, A. (2006). Peer-facilitated eating disorder prevention: A randomized effectiveness trial of cognitive dissonance and media advocacy. *The Journal of Counseling Psychology, 53,* 550–555. https://doi.org/10.1037/0022–0167.53.4.550

Bennis, W. (1975). *Leadership.* Cincinnati: University of Cincinnati.

Berger, M. (2002). Envy and generosity between co-therapists. *Group, 26,* 107–121. https://doi.org/10.1023/a:1015430913790

Bion, W. (1961). *Experiences in groups.* New York: Basic Books.

Boyatzis, R., and McKee, A. (2005). *Resonant leadership: Renewing yourself and connecting with others through mindfulness, hope, and compassion.* Boston: Harvard Business School Press.

Brack, A. B., Millard, M., and Shah, K. (2008). Are peer educators really peers? *Journal of American College Health, 56,* 566–568. https://doi .org/10.3200/jach.56.5.566–568

Braun, P. and Townley, J. (2015). The international student mentoring program. In Collier, P., *Developing effective student peer mentoring programs* (pp. 312–319). Sterling, VA: Stylus.

Brotherton, P. (2010). *Seating arrangements can affect group morale. T+D, 64,* 24. Retrieved from: https://www.td.org/Publications /Magazines/TD

Buote, V., Pancer, S. M., Pratt, M., Adams, G., Birnie-Lefcovitch, S., Polivy, J., and Wintre, M. G. (2007). The importance of friends: Friendships and adjustment among first-year university students. *Journal of Adolescent Research, 22,* 665–689. https://doi.org/10.1177 /0743558407306344

Burgoon, J. K. (2003). Spatial relationships in small groups. In R.Y. Hirokawa, R.S. Cathcart, L. A. Smaover, and L.D. Henman (Eds.), *Small group communication: Theory and practice* (pp. 85–96). Los Angeles: Roxbury.

Burn, S. M. (2004). *Group: Theory and practice.* Belmont, CA: Thompson.

Burns, J. M. (1978). *Leadership.* New York: Harper & Row.

Buss, D. M. (1990). The evolution of anxiety and social exclusion. *Journal of Social and Clinical Psychology, 9,* 196–210. https://doi.org/10.1521 /jscp.1990.9.2.196

Buss, D. M. (1991). Evolutionary personality psychology. *Annual Review of Psychology, 42,* 459–491. https://doi.org/10.1146/annurev.psych .42.1.459

Carns, A. W., Carns, M. R., and Wright, J. (1993). Student as para-professionals in four-year colleges and universities: Current practice compared to prior practice. *Journal of College Student Development, 34,* 358–363. Retrieved from https://eric.ed.gov /?id=EJ472307.

Cartwright, D. and Zander, A. F. (1968). *Group dynamics: Research and theory.* New York: Harper & Row.

Chun Chu, A. H. and Choi, J. N. (2005). Rethinking procrastination: Positive effects of "active" procrastination behaviors on attitudes and performance. *Journal of Social Psychology, 145,* 245–264. https://doi .org/10.3200/socp.145.3.245-264

Cohen, M. B. and DeLois, K. (2001). Training in Tandem: Co-facilitation and role modeling in a group work course. *Social Work with Groups, 24,* 21–36. https://doi.org/10.1300/j009v24n01_03

Collier, P. (2015). *Developing effective student peer mentoring programs.* Sterling, VA: Stylus.

Corey, M. S. and Corey, G. (2003). *Groups process and practice (6th ed.).* Pacific Grove, CA: Brooks.

Crocker, J. and Luhtanen, R. (1990). Collective self-esteem and ingroup bias. *Journal of Personality and Social Psychology, 58,* 60–67. https:// doi.org/10.1037//0022-3514.58.1.60

Cuseo, J. (2007). Seven central principles of student success: Key processes associated with positive student outcomes. *e-Source for College Transitions, 4(6),* 2, 3, 7. Retrieved from http://sc.edu/fye/esource /archive.html

Cuseo, J. (2010a). Peer power: Empirical evidence for the positive impact of peer interaction, support, and leadership. *e-Source for College Transitions, 7(4),* 4–6. Retrieved from http://sc.edu/fye/esource /archive.html

Cuseo, J. (2010b). Peer leadership: Definition, description, and classification. *e-Source for College Transitions 7(5),* 3–5. Retrieved from http://sc.edu/fye/esource/archive.html

Cuseo, J. (2010c). Peer Leadership: Situation-specific support roles. *e-Source for College Transitions, 7(6),* 4, 5, 8. Retrieved from http:// sc.edu/fye/esource/archive.html

Cutrona, C. E. (1982). Transition to college: Loneliness and the process of social adjustment. In L. A. Peplau and D. Perlman (Eds.), *Loneliness: A source book of current theory, research, and therapy* (pp. 291–309). New York: John Wiley & Sons.

Davidson, O. B., Feldman, D. B., and Margalit, M. (2012). A focused intervention for 1st-year college students: Promoting hope, sense of coherence, and self-efficacy. *Journal of Psychology, 146*, 333–352. https://doi.org/10.1080/00223980.2011.634862

de Grave, W. D., Zanting, A., Mansvelder-Longayroux, D. D., and Molenaar, W. M. (2014). Workshops and seminars: Enhancing effectiveness. In Steinert, Y. (Ed.) *Faculty development in the health professions: Innovation and change in professional education: Vol 11* (pp. 181–195). Dordrecht: Springer. https://doi.org/10.1007/978-94-007-7612-8_9.

Dennison, S. (2010). Peer mentoring: Untapped potential. *Journal of Nursing Education, 49*, 340–342. https://doi.org/10.3928/01484834-20100217-04.

Dick, B., Lessler, K., and Whiteside, K. (1980). A developmental framework for cotherapy. *International Journal of Group Psychotherapy, 30*, 273–285. Retrieved from http://dx.doi.org/10.1080/00207284.1980.11491692

Duba, J. D. (2004). Using silence: "Silence is not always golden." In L. Tyson, R. Pérusse, J. Whitledge, J. Duba, P. Neufeld, and J. DeVoss (Eds.), *Critical incidents in group counseling* (pp. 265–270). Alexandria, VA: American Counseling Association.

Eichler, M. (1987). Using structured group workshops to teach group process. *Teaching of Psychology, 14*, 42–44. https://doi.org/10.1207/s15328023top1401_12

Engleberg, I. N. and Wynn, D. R. (2013). *Working in groups.* Boston: Houghton Mifflin.

Erickson, E. (2015). Student veteran-focused program VETS to VETS program. In Collier, P., *Developing effective student peer mentoring programs* (pp. 218–223). Sterling, VA: Stylus.

Fall, K. A. and Wejnert, T. J. (2005). Co-leader stages of development: An application of Tuckman and Jensen (1977). *The Journal for Specialists in Group Work, 30*, 309–327. https://doi.org/10.1080/01933920500186530

Fee, R. L. and Tangney, J. P. (2000). Procrastination: A means of avoiding shame or guilt? *Journal of Social Behavior and Personality, 15,* 167–184. Retrieved from https://www.sbp-journal.com/index.php/sbp

Frank, J. D. and Ascher, E. (1951). Corrective emotional experiences in group therapy. *American Journal of Psychiatry, 108,* 126–131. https://doi.org/10.1176/ajp.108.2.126

Fuhriman, A. J. and Burlingame, G. M. (1990). Consistency of matter: A comparative analysis of individual and group process variables. *Counseling Psychologists, 18,* 6-63. https://doi.org/10.1177/0011000090181002

Gallogly, V. and Levine, B. (1979). Co-therapy. In B. Levine (Ed.), *Group psychotherapy: Practice and development* (pp. 296–305). Prospect Heights, IL: Waveland.

Gardner, J. W. (1990). *On Leadership.* New York: Free Press.

Garvin, C. and Reed, B. (1983). *Group work with women/group work with men: An overview of gender issues in social groupwork practice.* Abingdon, United Kingdom: Routledge.

Gladding, S. T. (2003). *Group work: A counseling specialty.* New Jersey: Prentice Hall.

Goldenberg, I. and Goldenberg, H. (2013). *Family therapy: An overview* (8th ed.). Pacific Grove, CA: Brookes/Cole.

Goleman, D., Boyatzis, R., and McKee, A., (2002). *The new leaders: Transforming the art of leadership into the science of results.* London, England: Little, Brown.

Gosser, D. K. and Roth, V. (1998). The workshop chemistry project: Peer-led team learning. *Journal of Chemical Education, 75,* 185–187. https://doi.org/10.1021/ed075p185

Greenfield, G., Keup, J., and Gardner, J. (2013). *Developing and sustaining successful first-year programs a guide for practitioners.* San Francisco: Jossey-Bass.

Hale, C. J., Hannum, J. W., and Espelage, D. L. (2005). Social support and physical health: The importance of belonging. *Journal of American College Health, 53,* 276–284. https://doi.org/10.3200/jach.53.6.276–284

Halgin, R. (1982). Using an experimental group to teach a group therapy course. *Teaching of Psychology, 9,* 188–189. https://doi.org/10.1207/s15328023top0903_18

Hall, E. T. (1982). *The hidden dimension.* New York: Doubleday.

Harper, M. S. and Allegretti, C. L. (2009a). Transition to University: An adjustment and retention program for first-year students. *E-source for College Transitions, 6(4),* 10–12. Retrieved from http://sc.edu/fye/esource/archive.html

Harper, M. S. and Allegretti, C. L. (2009b). Transition to University: *The impact of a first-year group experience on student outcomes and university fit.* Poster presentation at the International Conference on First-Year Experiences, Montreal, Canada.

Harper, M. S. and Allegretti, C. L. (2013). Expanding a peer-facilitation program beyond the fall term. *E-source for College Transitions, 11(1),* 16–17. Retrieved from http://sc.edu/fye/esource/archive.html

Harper, M. S. and Allegretti, C. L. (2015). Teaching group dynamics through an application-based learning approach. *Teaching of Psychology, 42,* 345–348. https://doi.org/10.1177/0098628315603251

Hefner, J. and Eisenberg, D. (2009). Social support and mental health among college students. *American Journal of Orthopsychiatry, 79,* 491–499. https://doi.org/10.1037/a0016918

Hendrick, C., Geisen, M., and Coy, S. (1974). The social ecology of free seating arrangements in a small group interaction context. *Sociometry, 37,* 262–274. https://doi.org/10.2307/2786380

Hibberd, J. M., Smith, D. L., and Wylie, D. M. (2006). In Hibberd, J. and Smith, D. (Eds.), *Leadership and leaders. Nursing leadership and management in Canada* (3rd ed., pp. 369–394). Toronto, ON: Elsevier Canada.

Homans, G. (1950). *The human group.* New York: Harcourt, Brace.

Homer, G. (1996). *The Odyssey* (Robert Fagles, trans.). New York: Penguin Books.

Howells, L. T. and Becker, S. W. (1962). Seating arrangements and leadership emergence. *Journal of Abnormal and Social Psychology, 62,* 148–150. https://doi.org/10.1037/h0040421

Hughes, K. (2011). Peer-assisted learning strategies in human anatomy and physiology. *American Biology Teacher, 73,* 144–147. https://doi.org/10.1525/abt.2011.73.3.5

Hulse-Killacky, D. (1996). Using the classroom as a group to integrate knowledge, skills, and supervised practice. *Journal for Specialists in*

Group Work, 21, 163–168. https://doi.org/10.1080/0193392960
8412246

Hunsberger, S., Pancer, S. M., Pratt, M., Rog, E., and Alisat, S. (2003). *Bridge over troubled water: Easing the transition to university.* Unpublished manuscript.

Jacobi, M. (1991). Mentoring and undergraduate academic success: A literature review. *Review of Educational Research, 61,* 505–532. https://doi.org/10.3102/00346543061004505

Johnson, D. W., and Johnson, F. P. (2013). *Joining together: Group theory and group skills* (11th ed.). Boston: Allyn and Bacon.

Johnson, V. K., Gans, S. E., Kerr, S., and LaValle, W. (2010). Managing the transition to college: Family functioning, emotion coping, and adjustment in emerging adulthood. *Journal of College Student Development, 51,* 607–621. https://doi.org/ 10.1353/csd.2010.0022

Kahn, E. W. (1996). Coleadership gender issues in group psychotherapy. In DeChant, B. (Ed.), *Women and group psychotherapy: Theory and practice* (pp. 442–462). New York: Guilford Press.

Kelly, F. (1972). Communicational significance of therapist proxemics cues. *Journal of Consulting and Clinical Psychology, 39,* 345. https://doi.org/10.1037/h0033423

Kivlighan, D. M., London, K., and Miles, J. R. (2011). Are two heads better than one? The relationship between number of group leaders and group members, and group climate and group member benefit from therapy. *Group Dynamics: Theory, Research and Practice, 16,* 1–13. https://doi.org/10.1037/a0026242

Knapp, H. (2007). *Therapeutic communication: Developing professional skills.* Los Angeles: Sage Publications.

Kouzes, J. M., and Posner, B. (2002). *The leadership challenge* (3rd ed.). San Francisco: Jossey-Bass.

Krause, K. and Freund, A. M. (2014). How to beat procrastination: The role of goal focus. *European Psychologist, 19,* 132–144. https://doi.org/10.1027/1016-9040/a000153

Kurzon, D. (2007). Towards a typology of silence. *Journal of Pragmatics, 39,* 1673–1688. DOI: 10.1016/j.pragma.2007.07.003

Ladany, N., Hill, C. E., Thompson, B. J., and O'Brien, K. M. (2004). Therapist perspectives on using silence in therapy: A qualitative study. *Counselling and Psychotherapy Research: Linking Research with Practice, 4,* 80–89. https://doi.org/10.1080/147331404123 31384088

Levine, J. M. and Moreland, R. L. (1994). Group socialization: Theory and research. *European Review of Social Psychology, 5,* 305-336. https://doi.org/10.1080/14792779543000093

Levitt, D. H. (2001). Active listening and counselor self-efficacy: Emphasis on one microskill in beginning counselor training. *Clinical Supervisor, 20,* 101–115. https://doi.org/10.1300/J001v20n02_09

Lockspeiser, T. M., O'Sullivan, P., Teherani, A., and Muller, J. (2008). Understanding the experience of being taught by peers: The value of social and cognitive congruence. *Advancement in Health Science, 12,* 123–134. https://doi.org/10.1007/s10459–006–9049–8

Ludin, W. H. and Aronov, B. M. (1952). Use of co-therapists in group psychotherapy. *Journal of Consulting Psychology, 16,* 76–80. https://doi.org/10.1037/h0055156

Luke, M. and Hackey, H. (2007). Group coleadership: A critical review. *Counseling Education & Supervision, 46,* 280-293. https://doi.org/10 .1002/j.1556–6978.2007.tb00032.x

Mattanah, J. F. (2016). *College student psychological experience: Exploring relational dynamics that predict success.* New York: Momentum Press.

Mattanah, J. F., Ayers, J., Brand, B., Brooks, L., Quimby, J., and McNary, S. (2010). A social support intervention to ease the college transition: Exploring main effects and moderators. *Journal of College Student Development, 51,* 93–108. https://doi.org/10.1353/ csd.0.0116

Mattanah, J. F., Brooks, L., Brand, B., Quimby, J., and Ayers, J.(2012). A social support intervention and academic achievement in college: Does perceived loneliness mediate the relationship? *Journal of College Counseling, 15,* 22–36. https://doi.org/10.1002/j.2161–1882.2012 .00003.x

Mattanah, J. F., Hancock, G. R., and Brand, B. L. (2004). Parental attachment, separation-individuation, and college student adjustment: A structural equation analysis of mediational effects. *Journal of Counseling Psychology, 51,* 213–225. https://doi.org/10.1037/0022 –0167.51.2.213

McGrath, J. E. (1984). *Groups: Interaction and performance.* Inglewood, N. J.: Prentice Hall.

Menneck, B. E., Hoffer, J. A., and Wynne, B. E. (1992). The implications of group development and history for group support system theory and practice. *Small Group Research, 23,* 524–572. https://doi.org/10.1177/1046496492234005

Michelini, R. L., Passalacqua, R., and Cusimano, J. (1976). Effects of seating arrangements on group participation. *Journal of Social Psychology, 99,* 179–186. https://doi.org/10.1080/00224545.1976.9924770

Miles, J. R. and Kivlighan, D. M. (2008). Team cognition in group interventions; The relation between co-leaders' shared mental models and group climate. *Group Dynamics: Theory, Research, and Practice, 12,* 191–209. https://doi.org/10.1037/1089-2699.12.3.191

Miles, J. R. and Kivlighan, D. M. (2010). Co-leader similarity and group climate in group interventions: Testing the co-leadership, team cognition-team diversity model. *Group Dynamics: Theory, Research, and Practice, 14,* 114–122. https://doi.org/10.1037/a0017503

Moore, N., Hickson, M., and Stacks, D. (2013). *Nonverbal communication: Studies and application,* (6th ed.). Oxford, England: Oxford University Press.

Moreland, R. L., and Levine, J. M. (1988). Group dynamics over time: Development and socialization in small groups. In J. E. McGrath (Ed.), *The social psychology of time: New perspectives* (pp. 151–181). Newbury Park, CA: Sage.

Moreno, J. K., Kramer, L., Scheidegger, C., and Weitzman, L. (2005). Gender and group psychotherapy: A review. *Group, 29,* 351–371. Retrieved from: http://link.springer.com/journal/10724

Newton, F. B., and Ender, S. C. (2010). *Students helping students: A guide for peer educations on college campuses* (2nd ed). San Francisco, CA: Jossey-Bass.

Nosko, A. and Wallace, R. (1997). Female/male co-leadership in groups. *Social Work with Groups, 20 (2),* 3–16. https://doi.org/10.1300/J009v20n02_02

Onwuegbuzie, A. J. (2004). Academic procrastination and statistics anxiety. *Assessment and Evaluation in Higher Education, 29,* 3–19. https://doi.org/10.1080/0260293042000160384

Ortiz, V. and Virnoche, M. (2015). Retention through an academic mentoring program. In Collier, P. (2015) *Developing effective student peer mentoring programs.* Sterling, VA: Stylus.

Pancer, S.M., Pratt, M., and Alisat, S. (2006). *T2U: A small group intervention to ease the transition of first-year students at university.* Paper presented at the biennial meeting of the Society for Research on Adolescence, San Francisco, California.

Pancer, S. M., Pratt, M., Hunsberger, B., and Alisat, S. (2004). Bridging troubled waters: Helping students make the transition from high school to university. *Guidance and Counselling, 19(4),* 184–190. Retreived from https://eric.ed.gov/?id=EJ739572

Pandey, V. A., Black, S. A., Lazaris, A. M., Allenberg, J. R., Eckstein, H. H., Hagmuller, G.W., Largiader, J., and Wolfe, J. H. N. (2005). Do workshops improve the technical skill of vascular surgical trainees? *European Journal of Vascular & Endovascular Surgery, 30,* 441–447. https://doi.org/10.1016/j.ejvs.2005.02.057

Paulson, I., Burroughs, J. C., and Gelb, C. B. (1976). Cotherapy: What is the crux of the relationship? *International Journal of Group Psychotherapy, 26,* 213–224. https://doi.org/10.1080/00207284.1976.11491933

Piper, W. E., Doan, B. D., Edwards, E. M., and Jones, B. D. (1979). Cotherapy behavior, group therapy process, and treatment outcome. *Journal of Consulting and Clinical Psychology, 47,* 1081–1089. https://doi.org/10.1037//0022–006X.47.6.1081

Pratt, M. W., Hunsberger, B., Pancer, S. M., Alisat, S., Bowers, C., Mackey, K., Ostaniewicz, A., Rog, E., Terzian, B., and Thomas, N. (2000). Facilitating the transition to university: Evaluation of a social support discussion intervention program. *Journal of College Student Development, 41,* 427–441.

Rankin, C. (2004). *Citizen: An American lyric.* Minneapolis, MN: Graywolf Press.

Riva, M. T. and Korinek, L. (2004). Teaching group work: Modeling group leader and member behaviors in the classroom to demonstrate group theory. *Journal for Specialists in Group Work, 29,* 55–63. https://doi.org/10.1007/978–3–7091–6663–5

Roberts, A. (1999). Homer's mentor duties fulfilled or misconstrued. Retrieved from http://www.nickols.us/homers_mentor.pdf

Ruthkosky, P. and Castano, S. (2007). First-year peer mentoring helps ease student transition to college. *e-Source for College Transitions, 5(1)*, 6, 9. Retrieved from http://tech.sa.sc.edu/fye/esource/files/ES_5-1_Sep07.pdf

Sanchez, R., Bauer, T., and Paronto, M. (2006). Peer-mentoring freshmen: Implications for satisfaction, commitment, and retention to graduation. *Academy of Management Learning and Education.* 5, 25–37. https://doi.org/10.5465/amle.2006.20388382

Schultz, W. (1966). *The interpersonal underworld.* Palo Alto, CA: Science and Behavior Books.

Scopelliti, M. and Tiberio, L. (2010). Homesickness in university students: The role of multiple place attachment. *Environment and Behavior, 42*, 335–350. doi:10.1177/0013916510361872

Silverstein, C. H. and Stang, D. J. (1976). Seating position and interaction in triads: A field study. *Sociometry, 39*, 166–170. https://doi.org/10.2307/2786217

Smith, T. (Ed.). (2013). *Undergraduate curricular peer mentoring programs: Perspectives on innovation by faculty, staff, and students.* Lanham, MD: Lexington Books.

Solomon, L. J. and Rothblum, E. D. (1984). Academic procrastination: Frequency and cognitive-behavioral correlates. *Journal of Counseling Psychology, 31*, 503–509. https://doi.org/10.1037/0022–0167.31.4.503

Sommer, R. (1967). Small group ecology. *Psychological Bulletin, 67*, 145–152. https://doi.org/10.2307/2786217

Sork, T. (1984). *Designing and implementing effective workshops: New directions for continuing education.* San Francisco: Jossey-Bass.

Steinert, Y. (2009). Twelve tips for conducting effective workshops. *Medical Teacher, 14*(2–3), 127–31. https://doi.org/10.3109/01421599 209079478

Steinzor, B. (1950). The spatial factors in face-to-face discussion groups. *Journal of Abnormal and Social Psychology, 45*, 552–555. https://doi.org/10.1037/h0061767

Sun, J., Hagedorn, L. S., and Zhang, Y. L. (2016). Homesickness at college: Its impact on academic performance and retention. *Journal of College Student Development, 57*, 943–957. https://doi.org/10.1353/csd.2016.0092

Swaab, R. I., Phillips, K. W., Diermeier, D., and Husted Medvec, V. (2008). The pros and cons of dyadic side conversations in

small groups. *Small Group Research, 39,* 372–390. https://doi
.org/10.1177/1046496408317044

Tajfel, H. (1981). *Human groups and social categories: Studies in social psychology.* Cambridge, England: Cambridge University Press.

Tajfel, H. and Turner, J. C. (1979). An integrative theory of intergroup conflict. In W. G. Austin, and S. Worchel (Eds.), *The social psychology of intergroup relations* (pp. 33–37). Monterey, CA: Brooks/Cole.

Terrion, J. and Leonard, D. (2007). A taxonomy of the characteristics of student peer mentors in higher education: Findings from a literature review. *Mentoring and Tutoring, 15,* 149–164. https://doi
.org/10.1080/13611260601086311

Thile, E. and Matt, G. (1995). The ethnic mentor undergraduate program: A brief description and preliminary findings. *Journal of Multicultural Counseling and Development, 23,* 116–126. https://doi.org/10
.1002/j.2161-1912.1995.tb00605.x

Thomson O' Brien, M. A., Freemantle, N., Oxman, A. D., Wolf, F., Davis, D. A., and Herrin, J. (2001). Continuing education meetings and workshops: Effects on professional practice and health care outcomes. *Cochrane Database of Systematic Reviews, 2,* CD003030. https://doi.org/10.1002/14651858.CD003030

Thurber, C. A. and Walton, E. A. (2012). Homesickness and adjustment in university students. *Journal of American College Health, 60,* 1–5. https://doi.org/10.1080/07448481.2012.673520

Tice, D. and Baumeister, R. F. (1997). Longitudinal study of procrastination, performance, stress, and health: The cost and benefits of dawdling. *Psychological Science, 8,* 454–458. https://doi.org/10.1111
/j.1467-9280.1997.tb00460.x

Tinto, V. (1999). Taking retention seriously: Rethinking the first year of college. NACADA, 19(2), 5–9. https://doi.org/10.12930/0271
−9517-19.2.5

Tinto, V. (2016). How to improve student persistence and completion. *Inside Higher Ed.* Retrieved from: https://www.insidehighered.com
/views/2016/09/26/how-improve-student-persistence-and
-completion-essay

Tomsich, E. A., Schaible, L. M., Rennison, C. M., and Gover, A. R. (2013). Violent victimization and hooking up among strangers and acquaintances on an urban campus: An exploratory study. *Criminal Justice Studies: A Critical Journal of Crime, Law, and Society, 26,* 433–454. https://doi.org/10.1080/1478601X.2013.842564

Tuckman, B. (1965). Developmental sequence in small groups. *Psychological Bulletin, 63,* 384–399. https://doi.org/10.1037/h0022100

Tuckman, B. W., and Jensen, M. A. C. (1977). Stages of small-group development revisited. *Group & Organization Management, 2,* 419–427. https://doi.org/105960117700200404

Upcraft, M. L., Gardner, J. N., and Barefoot, B. O. (Eds.). (2007). *Challenging and supporting the first-year students: A handbook for improving the first year of college.* San Francisco: Jossey-Bass Publishers.

Vannicelli, M. (1992). *Removing the roadblocks: Group psychotherapy with substance abusers and family members.* New York: Guilford Press.

Walker, D. and Verklan, T. (2016). Peer mentoring during practicum to reduce anxiety in first-semester nursing students. *Journal of Nursing Education, 55,* 651–654. https://doi.org/10.3928/01484834-20161011–08

Watt, S. E. and Badger, A. J. (2009). Effects of social belonging on homesickness: An application of the belongingness hypothesis. *Personality and Social Psychology Bulletin, 35,* 516–530. https://doi.org/10.1177/0146167208329695

Wheelan, S. (2005). *Group processes: A developmental perspective.* Boston: Addison-Wesley.

White H. R., Labouvie E. W., and Papadaratsakis V. (2005). Changes in substance use during the transition to adulthood: A comparison of college students and their noncollege age peers. *Journal of Drug Issues, 35,* 281–306. https://doi.org/10.1177/002204260503500204

White, H. R., McMorris, B. J., Catalano, R. F., Fleming, C. B., Haggerty, K. P., and Abbott, R. D. (2005). Increases in alcohol and marijuana use during the transition out of high school into emerging adulthood: The effects of leaving home, going to college, and high school protective factors. *Journal of Studies on Alcohol and Drugs, 67,* 810–22. https://doi.org/10.15288/jsa.2006.67.810 3.

Whitworth, L., Kinsey-House, K., Kimsey-House, H., and Sandahl, P. (2007). *Co-active coaching: New skills for coaching people toward success in work and life.* Mountain View, CA: Davies-Black Publishing.

Wintre, M. G., Knoll, G. M., Pancer, S. M., Pratt, M. W., Polivy, J., Birnie-Lefcovitch, S., and Adams, G. R. (2008). The Transition to University: The Student-University Match (SUM). *Journal of Adolescent Research, 23*, 745–769. https://doi.org/10.1177/0743558408325972

Wolf, T. M., Scurria, P. L., and Webster, M. G. (1998). A four-year study of anxiety, depression, loneliness, social support and perceived mistreatment in medical students. *Journal of Health Psychology, 3*, 125–136. https://doi.org/10.1177/135910539800300110

Worschel, S., Coutant-Sassic, D., and Grossman, M. (1992). A developmental approach to group dynamics: A model and illustrative research. In S. Worschel, W. Wood, and J. Simpson (Eds.), *Group process and productivity* (pp. 181–202). Newbury Park, CA: Sage.

Yalom, I. D. (1975). *The theory and practice of group psychotherapy.* New York: Basic Books.

Yalom, I. D., and Leszcz, M. (2005). *The theory and practice of group psychotherapy* (5th ed.). New York, NY: Basic Books.

About the Author

Melinda S. Harper, PhD, is professor of psychology at Queens University of Charlotte. She introduced and continues to co-direct the Transition to University (T2U) program. She and her co-author, Dr. Christine Allegretti, have published a number of articles and presented empirical research about the T2U program. In addition to her teaching and research, Dr. Harper also maintains an active clinical practice as a psychologist and partner of Charlotte Psychotherapy & Consultation Group. Her primary clinical focus is on assisting adolescents and young adults with normative transitions in their lives, including the transition from high school to college and from college to the workforce.

Christine L. Allegretti, PhD, is professor of psychology at Queens University of Charlotte. Along with Dr. Melinda Harper, she introduced and continues to co-direct the Transition to University (T2U) program. Her research interests are in the areas of critical thinking, loneliness, and first-year student adjustment. In addition to teaching in the Department of Psychology, she has taught in the first-year core curriculum program, organized a first-year experience program, and served as chair of psychology and chair of social sciences at Queens. She was also the recipient of the William S. Lee Teaching Award at Queens University of Charlotte.

Index

OTHER TITLES IN OUR PSYCHOLOGY COLLECTION

www.ingramcontent.com/pod-product-compliance
Lightning Source LLC
Chambersburg PA
CBHW061609220326
41598CB00024BC/3505